CALLOWAY COUNTY PUBLIC LIBRARY
710 Main Street
MURRAY, KY 42071

D1489613

EARLY AMERICAN HOMES

The Pleasures of Christmas

Copyright © 1996 by
Early American Homes
All rights reserved under International and
Pan-American Copyright Conventions.

No part of this book may be reproduced or transmitted in any form or by any means electronic
or mechanical including photocopying, recording, or by any information storage and retrieval system,
without permission in writing from the publisher.

This 1996 edition is published by Glorya Hale Books,
an imprint of Random House Value Publishing, Inc.,
40 Engelhard Avenue, Avenel, New Jersey 07001.

Random House
New York • Toronto • London • Sydney • Auckland
http://www.randomhouse.com/

Design by Liz Trovato
Production supervision by Michael Siebert

Printed and bound in the United States of America

Library of Congress Cataloging-in-Publication Data
Early American Homes' The pleasures of Christmas /
edited by Mimi Handler.
p. cm.
ISBN 0–517–14926–5 (hard cover)
1. Christmas decorations. 2. Handicraft.
3. Christmas cookery. 4. Entertaining.
I. Handler, Mimi. II. Early American Homes.
TT900.C4E365 1996   96–17672
745.594'12'0973——dc20   CIP
8 7 6 5 4 3 2 1

EARLY AMERICAN HOMES

The Pleasures of Christmas

Edited by Mimi Handler

GHB

GLORYA HALE BOOKS
NEW YORK · AVENEL

Contents

Introduction

Looking back to an America when things seemed simpler, more connected, is particularly appropriate to the celebration of Christmas. It is the theme of this book, which is entirely about Christmas in early American homes—the kind of homes that long ago included three or four generations who made most of their Christmas pleasures themselves, regarded an orange in the toe of a stocking as an indispensable gift and traditions as an integral part of keeping Christmas.

Some of the pictures were taken in historic homes (which, after all, were somebody's home once). More often, though, the rooms pictured in these pages are in some of today's best-preserved, thoroughly lived in homes. Still others are in new houses built in early American styles, with the steeply pitched roof lines, classic doorways, ornamental woodwork, and paint colors directly descended from an American past rich with detail and resourcefulness. New or old, every one of them offers an invitation to visit for a while, contemplate the season's historic connections, and bring them, like gifts, to your own home for Christmas.

We hope some of the ideas will spark your imagination and involve your hands. The notion, for example of hanging one shaped cookie in each pane of a many-paned window, is the essence of simplicity and goes way back in time. Timelessness doesn't necessarily mean complicated or expensive. A small blue and white china bowl heaped with four or five gilded Osage oranges or fragrant golden quince, sprigged with glossy boxwood, for example; a wreath of your own devising studded with lady apples and baby's breath; garnet cranberries strung and looped amidst sprays of long-leaf pine on a staircase; the grace-ful, urn-shaped pineapple in a place of honor, are all old tradi-tions ready to become your own.

New England Puritans banned Christmas, but it came anyway, later on. The Old World's Christmas traditions arrived with immi-grants, successive waves of English, Scotch-Irish, German, Scandinavian, Polish, Italian, so many cultural and family tradi-tions, and intermixed into what have become something else again, like no other, distinctly American ones. It has always been the American genius to freely adapt, combine, and transform cus-toms; no sooner did Saint Nicholas come to America than he began changing into our own Santa Claus—the American one—bigger, heartier, more fun. Our Christmas tables offer again what the family enjoyed for the first time last year—or a hundred years ago, great-grandmother's remembered recipe (or somebody else's great-grandmother's recipe).

On these pages are the historical reasons (as if you needed reasons) for such pretty traditions as table-top trees and their decorations, Christmas cards, the old penny toys, and glittering ornaments that give an antique luster to the season. You'll find recipes from homes, not from test kitchens, and ideas that may prompt you to look at the late summer garden, the nearest win-ter woodland, even those crisp bunches of hydrangeas on an autumn bush, in a speculative, planning-for-Christmas way.

Here are old ways to decorate that will never go out of style because they are old-fashioned to begin with. The pleasures of Christmas have a long and richly diverse heritage. This book makes it possible for you to add some of them to your own.

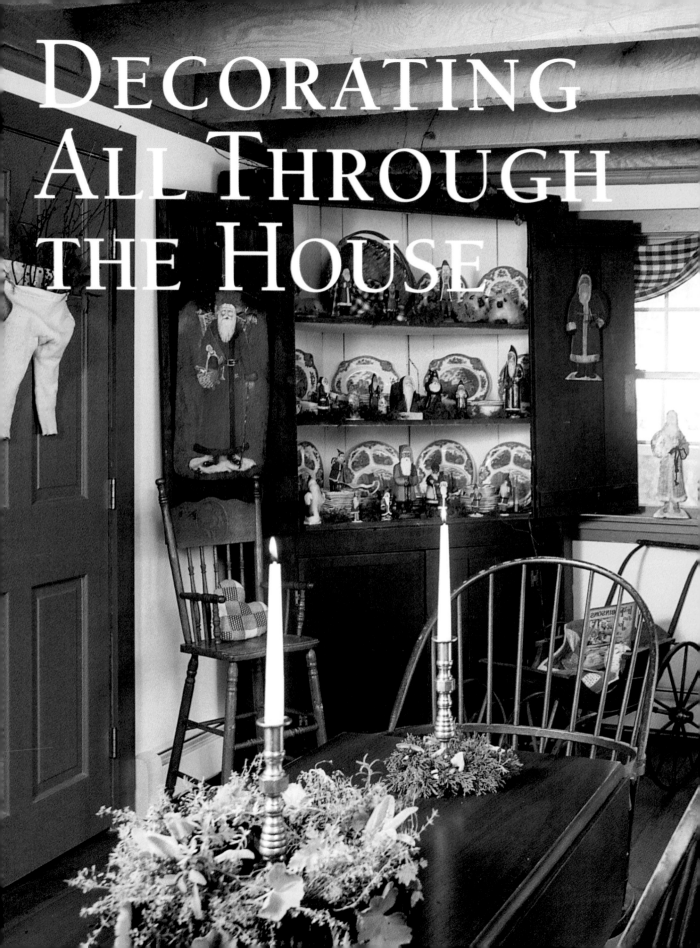

Decorating
All Through
the House

Some people just decorate a tree at Christmas, hang a wreath on the front door, arrange some pine boughs and holly in a pretty vase, and then, after admiring their handiwork, go about their celebrations. Other people decorate their homes as if they were trees. Each room is a kind of branch waiting for its holiday trimmings. They often have trees in every room, chains of snowmen and angels, inventive and ever-changing decorations, ornaments that friends have made, and ornaments that have made friendships.

The beautifully decorated room shown here is the keeping room of a stone farmhouse in Pennsylvania, built about 1750 on part of a William Penn land grant. (A keeping room is a multipurpose family room that runs the width of an eighteenth-century center-chimney house. Although it is not evident in this photograph, the focus of the room is a large fireplace.)

During the holidays this room is resplendent with old and new decorations. The tall, bushy Christmas tree is filled with antique ornaments and surrounded with antique toys within a miniature fence. The Santa breadboard hanging on the cupboard, and most of the painted figures in the room, are relatively new. In the corner cupboard old and new Santa figures in their bright red coats contrast with a collection of Johnson Brothers Castles of England plates. The marvelous nineteenth-century baby carriage is filled with antique books and toys.

In the kitchen of the same eighteenth-century farmhouse, right, a ham roasts on the hearth, while soup simmers in a pot hanging from a crane over the coals. The settle table (which can be turned into a bench when it is not in use), is laden with some of the traditional foods of Christmas—roast goose, home-baked breads, and gingerbread men. Clusters of chili peppers, cranberries, and bunches of bay leaves were strung to make the garland that hangs on the mantel.

When the doors of the tin-paneled jelly cupboard are open, below, some red apples, fresh greens, with sticks of cinnamon tucked in here and there, and a string of paper-doll angels give it a jolly Christmas look.

CALLOWAY COUNTY PUBLIC LIBRARY
710 Main Street
MURRAY, KY 42071

The rooms shown here are in a house that is decorated from attic to basement during the holidays. The shelf, at one end of the family room, left, holds an array of handmade wooden Santas—a different one (or two or three) are added each year—in a woodland of short pine boughs. A garland, accented with deep red apples and intervals of red, green, and gold striped ribbon, is hung across the wall. The same ribbon makes the bows on the wreath above the shelf and the one that is hung inside the window.

Informality, even an American primitive look, characterizes the dining room decorations, above. A pine garland, wrapped and tied with brown Kraft paper rush, is hung just below the mantelpiece. The wreath above the mantel is tied with the same material. The collection of crocks, supplemented with charming angels, fits in with the other decorations.

In this late nineteenth-century house in York, Maine, the comfortable living room was added to the kitchen in the back of the house. A focal point all through the year is the interesting collection of new folk art game boards arranged on the wall. A pot of bright poinsettia, a garland of pine boughs hung over the doors to the deck, and a Christmas tree in the corner dress the room for the holidays. The tree, trimmed with homemade, many-pointed Moravian stars, heart-shaped ornaments, candles in weighted holders, and strings of popcorn, is surrounded by a collection of winsome bears.

Spices simmering in a kettle on the antique wood stove, above, fill the kitchen, and much of the house, with a delicious fragrance. On the antique commode chair a worn wooden bucket filled with pine boughs and holly adds a delightful touch of Christmas.

The keeping room, left, in a wonderful limestone house in Berks County, Pennsylvania, built in 1751, is imaginatively decorated with boughs of cedar. These trees, which grow in fence rows in southeastern Pennsylvania, have long been the traditional Christmas trees of the thrifty Pennsylvania Germans. The pineapple in the centerpiece on the table is a graceful shape in its own right as well as being a traditional symbol of hospitality.

Hung By the Chimney

No matter which room of the house a fireplace is in, it is almost always the focal point—and nothing adds a more festive touch than a mantel decorated for Christmas.

In the summer kitchen of an eighteenth-century New England house, left, the large brick fireplace is surrounded with an eye-catching garland of laurel leaves, winter berries, and gingerbread people dressed in piped icing. A garland of boxwood and crabapples hangs in swags around the entire room. (Taking his ease on an antique step-back Windsor chair before the fire is Lexington, said to be one of the three fattest cats in Massachusetts.)

What looks like a fireplace in the kitchen of the eighteenth-century house, right, was a practical and interesting solution for a boring wall. It conceals an enormous storage closet, and the mantelpiece above the nonworking fireplace provides a place to display family treasures, including a variety of old wooden spindles from a textile factory, which the children use to blow soap bubbles. The pine garland under the "mantel" is interlaced with dried apple rings, red apples, gingerbread cookies, and silver bells.

For almost thirty years, the fireplace in the keeping room of the eighteenth-century house, right, was hidden behind a wall of knotty pine paneling; the chimney cupboard door was found stashed in the barn. The present owners returned the fireplace to its former splendor and at Christmas each year they hang a swag of old-fashioned, homey decorations above it. Christmas elves, suspended in the recessed corners of the step chimney, ride the warm fragrant updraft.

Adorning the mantel, below, in an 1834 fieldstone farmhouse in central Pennsylvania is an antique Noah's ark and many of the animals marching two by two. The swags of pine boughs, caught up with a spray of holly, and the bright red candles and red ribbon on the grapevine wreath add color and enhance the whole arrangement.

This mantel shelf in a master bedroom is decorated for Christmas with garlands of crimson cranberries, short pine boughs, red candles in gleaming brass candlesticks, and a collection of small Santas. The unusual wreath of eucalyptus and wild rose hips is very much part of the arrangement.

Windows on Christmas

It was in the windows of homes that Christmas decorations were first displayed. A welcoming candle in the window, particularly at Christmas, is an old custom. With the addition of fresh greenery and dried herbs, fruit, and flowers, windows became increasingly festive during the holidays. Wreaths were hung in windows in the eighteenth century, before they were hung on doors and well before Christmas trees became commonplace.

In the middle of the nineteenth century, people began to fill every nook and cranny of their homes with holiday decorations. Garlands of greens were draped over portraits; leaves and fresh fruit were arranged in transoms; and live bedecked trees, illuminated with candles, were the glittering focus of the season. Nevertheless, the window remained a special place for festive ornamentation. Today the tradition continues of using windows as settings for wreaths, garlands, and arrangements of special collections, toys, and cookies on the sills.

The decorated windows, right, cast a holiday spell over the living room. In the bay window at the far end of the room, a Canada goose decoy keeps watch over a collection of brass candlesticks. Above the window, children's horns and a red bow anchor the swag of cedar, juniper, and balsam greens. The wreaths, made with spruce and tied with bright red ribbons, are hung inside the windows.

Back-lit with natural light during the day, and lit from inside at night, a window provides a splendid background for all kinds of ornaments and decorations. In the large window opposite, cookies, among the oldest of homemade Christmas ornaments, are framed within individual panes in the Pennsylvania German tradition.

The narrow window, right, in the pantry of an old house in Plymouth, Massachusetts, is decorated with a rope of pine hung with bunches of dried flowers and baby's breath tied with blue moire ribbon. On the table in front of the window spicy potpourri and a basket of pomanders add a delicious scent of Christmas.

The simple arrangement, far right, of flowers, toys, and a vine wreath tied with a bright red ribbon bestows holiday cheer on the winter view.

Collections set up with playful ease often characterize holiday decorating. The collection of tin cookie cutters mounted on a stand, for example, makes a sculpture of folk designs in the window on the bottom far right. The grapevine wreath, pine boughs, candlestick, and bright touches of red make the arrangement quite festive.

On the windowsill below, with pine boughs behind them, Santas and sheep congregate in a whimsical tableau.

During the holiday season, over the windows of the elegant dining room in a refurbished nineteenth-century house in York, Maine, simple swags of long-leaf pine and crimson berries echo the year 'round stencil of leaves and strawberries. The pyramid centerpiece on the table, an artful arrangement of pine boughs, variegated holly leaves, and shiny red apples topped with a pineapple, is easy to make and would be a delightful addition to any holiday table.

The pyramid shape was extremely popular in early America. In the photograph above, a pyramid of Greek cookies, called Kourambiedes, creates a delicious snowy mountain made all the more attractive by holly leaves and berries.

Decorated Stairways

The stairway is often the first thing that is seen when the front door is opened. When the newel post and banisters are decorated for the holidays it adds a welcoming note to all who enter. When decorating a stairway, be sure to do so in such a way that people going up or down the stairs can still get a firm grip on the banister.

The charming bouquet of nandina berries, golden yarrow flowers, and boxwood looks wonderful on the newel post below. Such an arrangement is not difficult to make. The base is a Styrofoam cube into which the stems of the flowers are pushed.

A garland of pine, yellow dried yarrow flowers, and bright red ribbons adorn the banister of the staircase on the right. Stools of varying heights next to the stairs hold pots of poinsettias in full bloom, which add a cheerful accent.

The front hall stairway, far right, is hung with an unusual calico swag of large red bows and soft sculpture. Pine boughs hang gracefully from the newel post, and some are tucked into the swag. At the top of the stairs Raggedy Ann and a small friend survey the scene below.

Welcoming Wreaths

A wreath on the front door during the holiday season greets everyone who passes the house or comes for a visit. Front door wreaths seem such nice, friendly decorations that it is not unusual to see them up well after the holiday season, or to see a Christmas wreath replaced with one made of materials that are not associated with the holiday.

A wreath can be made of a small garland, formed into a circle and the two ends joined with floral wire. The magnificent Douglas fir wreath, top left, is decorated with dried peach hydrangea, peach yarrow, artichokes, okra pods, fresh eucalyptus leaves, and pine cones. A wreath of dried flowers and vegetables is best hung on an outside door that has a substantial overhang so it is protected from rain and snow, which could destroy it. This wreath would look marvelous indoors, particularly centered on a wall above a fireplace.

The simple wreath at left is made of blue spruce, boxwood, and clusters of apples. The pineapple is a traditional American symbol of hospitality and becomes more decoration than dessert at Christmas, appearing on mantels, newel posts, and wreaths. This one is on the door of a red New England barn.

The stunning wreath right decorates the front door of a house in Chester County, Pennsylvania. It is made of Douglas fir, magnolia leaves, boxwood, red pepper berries, pine cones, oranges, gold yarrow flowers, and eucalyptus.

Wreaths for All Seasons

A wreath adds a nice decorating accent inside as well as outside the house. It is not difficult to make a wreath, particularly if you use a straw or Styrofoam ring as a base. The large wreath right is made of dried materials so it will look fresh and pretty for many months. You can substitute any dried or fresh leaves, flowers, or berries you prefer. You might want to make two—one for yourself, the other as a gift.

This enchanting wreath, decorated with soft-sculpture hearts and a little bird made of homespun cloth, is tied appropriately with a gingham bow.

This unusual spruce and pine wreath above, is embellished with lemons, dried yarrow, and dried pods from the sweet gum tree.

To make our wreath, you can substitute dried flowers and berries of your choice and follow our instructions.

1. Pull Spanish moss around circumference of wreath, covering the top and sides as evenly as possible.

Materials

14-inch straw wreath

Spanish moss

Floral wire

Fern pins, about 150

Aleene's Tacky Glue

Twigs

Eucalyptus, 2 branches

Pepper berries, rose hips, or any red berries

Sweet Annie

Dried white flowers (acroclinium is a good choice)

2. Wrap floral wire around the wreath to hold moss in place.

3. Starting at any point and working in one direction—attach dried materials by grouping different bunches (except berries), securing each bunch with a fern pin.

4. Continue to pin bundles of different combinations of materials in rows across the top of the wreath and into the inside curve. As you move around the wreath, additional bundles should just cover previous pins.

5. When the wreath is half covered, step back and review the overall appearance for balance.

6. When the wreath is completed, dip pepper berries in glue and push in close to wreath's base for color contrast. Pepper berries are brittle and tend to break when secured by a fern pin. Other berries such as bittersweet or rose hips can be substituted and incorporated in the bundles originally pinned to the wreath.

Pineapple and Pomander Pyramid

The pineapple is a traditional symbol of hospitality and quite appropriately tops this pretty, scented centerpiece. In the early days of the nation, seafarers would often return from their voyages with strange and exotic "curiousities," like the pineapple. The naturally graceful, urn-shaped fruit, golden and coppery green in color, is a classic decorative motif in wood, metal, printed or stitched on cloth, even stenciled on walls.

In this arrangement, the pineapple is surrounded by clove-studded, cinnamon-scented oranges, or pomanders, which add a spicy aroma to the holiday table.

Instructions

Mid-November is the best time to make the pomanders so they will "ripen" by the time you need them in December. With the black marker, make decorative star, spiral, and striped designs on the oranges. With the skewer or knitting needle, pierce the skins of the oranges, following the black outlines. Leave a little space between each hole. Insert the stems of the cloves into the holes in the oranges.

In a small bowl, mix together the cinnamon and the orris root. Pour the mixture into a plastic bag. Put one orange at a time into the bag and shake gently until it is well-covered with the powder. Place the oranges on a tray large enough to hold them in one layer. Leave them in a cool, dark place, turning them every few days.

When you are ready to arrange the pyramid, brush the excess powder from the surface of the oranges. Arrange them in the metal pyramid form. Place the pineapple on the top of the form. Tuck pine boughs into the spaces around the fruit.

Materials

Fine-point black marker
11 medium-size, thin-skinned oranges
Small metal skewer or a knitting needle
Whole cloves
½ cup powdered orris root
½ cup powdered cinnamon
Medium-size plastic bag
Tray, large enough to hold the oranges in one layer
Large, well-shaped pineapple
Short pine boughs
Metal pyramid form

A Tree of Herbs and Flowers

This tree of dried herbs and flowers is easy to make and looks quite impressive as a centerpiece on a buffet table, or on a table anywhere in the house. The materials are available from large craft stores. You can use any dried materials you like including dried roses, eucalyptus, and hydrangea. Although the tree will stand by itself, it does look lovely in a low container like the stenciled Shaker-style box shown here.

Instructions

Evenly distribute the artemisia on the tree, trimming it to the desired length as you proceed from the top to the bottom and using a hot-glue gun to secure it.

Next add the mountain mint, sunflowers, red pepper berries, tansy, and any additional herbs and flowers of your choice. Attach each item separately to the tree with hot glue. Be sure to fill in any empty spots.

Materials
18-inch twig tree
Artemisia
Mountain mint
Sunflowers
Red pepper berries
Tansy
Dried herbs and flowers
Hot-glue gun

A Marzipan Tree

This slender centerpiece is not difficult to make. The tree can stand right on the table, on a pretty plate, or on a stemmed compote. You can buy the almond paste. You may even prefer to buy the marzipan fruit, although it is fun to make.

Materials

Green Styrofoam pyramid

Boxwood sprigs, 2 to 3 inches

Toothpicks

Marzipan fruit

1 cup almond paste

1 cup powdered sugar

A few drops of rose water,
    orange extract, or brandy

Whole cloves

Angelica

Food coloring

2 cups granulated sugar (optional)

Instructions

Stick the ends of the boxwood sprigs into the Styrofoam pyramid, covering it completely. Use toothpicks to attach the fruit to the tree. To avoid the toothpicks coming through the fruit, break them in half before using them.

To make the marzipan fruit: Combine the almond paste, sugar, and rose water. On a marble slab or a chilled platter, knead for about 20 minutes, or until the mixture is smooth and soft enough to shape. Pinch off small pieces of the marzipan and add food coloring appropriate to the fruit you are molding. With your fingers, shape the marzipan into tiny fruits. To add texture to an orange shape, roll it lightly over a grater. Form peaches and plums by pressing two round balls together. Mimic the fruit stem and base by attaching a whole clove to the bottom of the fruit so the star point is visible, and another to the top of the fruit so the stem is visible. Use bits of angelica for the leaves. Brush the fruit with a little red food coloring to add a faint blush. Dry the fruit on a wire rack.

To make the fruit glisten, in a saucepan combine the granulated sugar with ½ cup of water. Cook over moderate heat, stirring until the sugar is dissolved, then bring to a boil of 223 degrees on a candy thermometer. Remove the pan from the heat and set aside until the syrup is cold. Carefully pour the syrup over each piece of marzipan fruit on the rack, coating it completely.

Let the fruit stand until the surfaces are dry and hard.

Swan Topiary

This delightful swan topiary is not difficult or expensive to make. All the materials are available from craft shops and garden centers. The amount of peat moss, sheet moss, and ivy you will require depends on the size of the topiary form you choose.

Although the topiary is a bit large for a centerpiece at a sit-down meal, it is perfect for a buffet table. It would also grace a table in an entrance hall or in the living room. Perhaps the nicest thing about this topiary is that, watered and misted regularly, it will last long after the holidays are over.

Materials
Sphagnum peat moss
Swan metal topiary form
Sheet moss
Nylon fishing line
English ivy
Fern pins or small hairpins
Aluminum foil
Sculpey III modeling compound, tan
Black acrylic paint, optional

You Will Also Need:
Hot-glue gun
Paint brush
Shallow tray, large enough to hold
    the topiary
Pebbles, to line the tray

Instructions
Soak the peat moss until it is thoroughly wet. Squeeze out most of the water and stuff the damp moss firmly into the swan form. Cover the outside of the form, except the area where the beak will go, with sheet moss, securing it with the fishing line.

To plant the ivy, poke a hole through the sheet moss into the main part of the form. Slip the rooted ivy, preferably with a little soil attached, into the hole. Arrange the ivy runners around the swan and out to the tail. Continue planting the ivy until the form is well covered. Fasten the ivy runners to the moss with fern pins.

Push more peat moss around the roots if necessary.

To make the beak, fold a 6-inch-square sheet of aluminum foil in half. Form the foil into a cone shape. Cover the foil with Sculpey so it resembles a beak. Bake according to the manufacturer's instructions. If desired, when the cone is cool, paint it black. Using the hot-glue gun, glue the beak in place.

Put the topiary on a shallow tray lined with pebbles and filled with water.

To care for the topiary, never allow the peat moss to dry out. Occasionally dunk the topiary in a bucket of water, or water gently. Mist the surface every day. As the ivy grows repin the runners to the sheet moss. Pinch back the leaf-bud tips so the cover will remain thick. Inspect the topiary for infestations of scale, to which ivy is susceptible. Spray with insecticide if necessary.

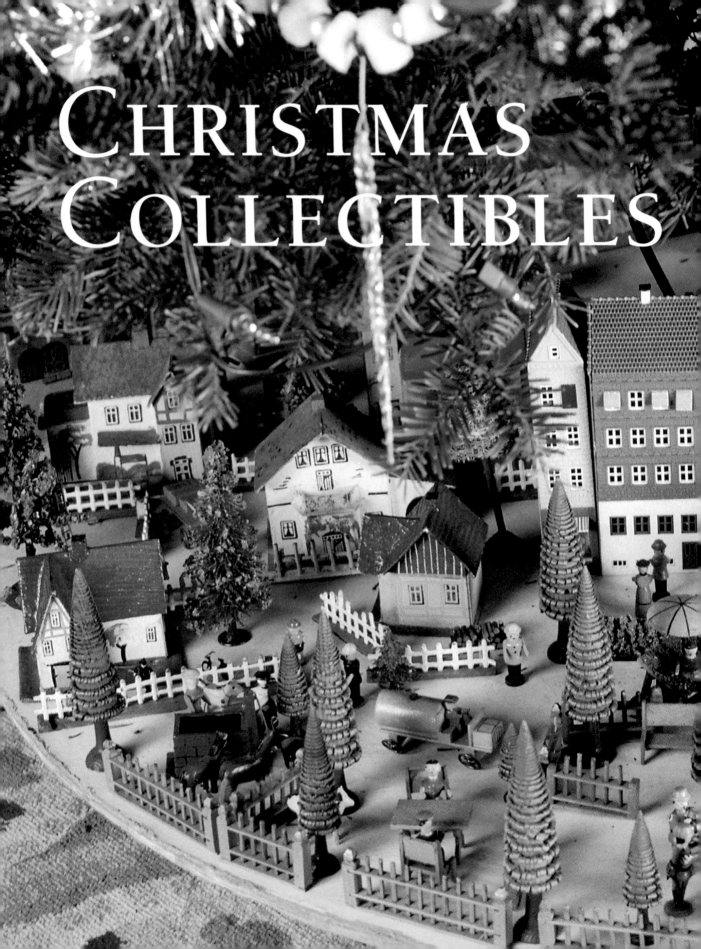

CHRISTMAS
COLLECTIBLES

*A*ll year 'round, Christmas is not far from the thoughts of the many people who are always looking for Christmas collectibles. Of course, most people are really Christmas collectors. They wait eagerly for the approach of the holidays so they can take that large box of familiar ornaments from the attic or the basement and delight once more in the memories so many of them evoke.

Then, in January, when the box is carefully repacked, there are almost always a few new ornaments and, perhaps, an irresistible antique Santa. And so the collection grows. Whether you buy your own holiday trimmings or have inherited some spectacular ornaments, years of affectionate use give them all special meaning.

This charming miniature village is the epitome of Christmas collectibles. The tiny pieces were bought in the 1920s, for pennies, for two New England sisters who continued to put them under their tree until just a few years ago. Now the village can be seen every year under the Christmas tree at the Whaling Museum in New Bedford, Massachusetts.

Collectible Santas

For Christmas collectors, Santa Claus in his many forms is the star of the season. There are rare, old, carved figures of Saint Nicholas, early Santa postcards and greeting cards, Santa candy containers and lanterns, Santa toys, and exquisite, handmade modern Santas, which have already become collectibles.

Santa himself is, quite properly, portrayed in many guises. He came to America as Saint Nicholas and quickly found the first of his new identities when he became Sante Klaas in the dialect of the earliest Dutch settlers, who pictured him as tall, thin, and stately. In 1809, Washington Irving described him as a jovial Dutch settler with presents in the pockets of his wide breeches. Clement C. Moore, in the poem "A Visit from St. Nicholas,"

which he wrote for his children in 1823, portrayed St. Nick as a jolly and rotund elf, dressed him in fur from head to foot, and gave him a white beard, a red nose, twinkling eyes, and a sleigh drawn by reindeer.

In parts of Germany after the Reformation, Saint Nicholas was replaced by Kris Kringle (the Christ Child or Christkindl), the angel-like bearer of gifts. In America, Kris Kringle, too, was replaced by Santa Claus.

All the Santas below are German and all are candy containers, with the exception of the two heads on the far left. They are lanterns which hold candles; the light glows through their eyes and mouths. The candy containers were selected to show the enormous range of expression, detail, interpretation, and even color in these depictions of Father Christmas.

People began sending greeting cards at Christmas in the mid-nineteenth century. In England, by the early 1860s, Christmas cards were being produced commercially and the custom of sending hand-printed greetings became increasingly popular. In 1895, Frances Cleveland, the wife of the president, Grover Cleveland, ordered thousands of cards, which were reported to be "unequaled for chaste simplicity and good taste."

Most of the early cards were single-fold or had light cardboard covers that enclosed a thinner sheet of paper that held the greeting. There was a holiday motif on the front cover and Santa Claus was a favorite subject. He was usually portrayed as a beatific grand-fatherly figure, as on the cards opposite, and quite unlike his stern-looking, three-dimensional counterparts below.

The collection of Santas, in a nineteenth-century hanging cupboard, is quite eclectic. The silver papier-mâché figure, far right on the bottom shelf, is the oldest. The newest figure is the Santa and sleigh, which is made of celluloid and dates from the 1930s.

There are all kinds of Santa collectibles. One that is particularly interesting is the chocolate mold, right. This Santa is a fraction under three feet tall, probably the height of Clement Moore's "jolly old elf." It was made by the firm of Anton Reiche, of Dresden, Germany, which was active from 1870 until 1930.

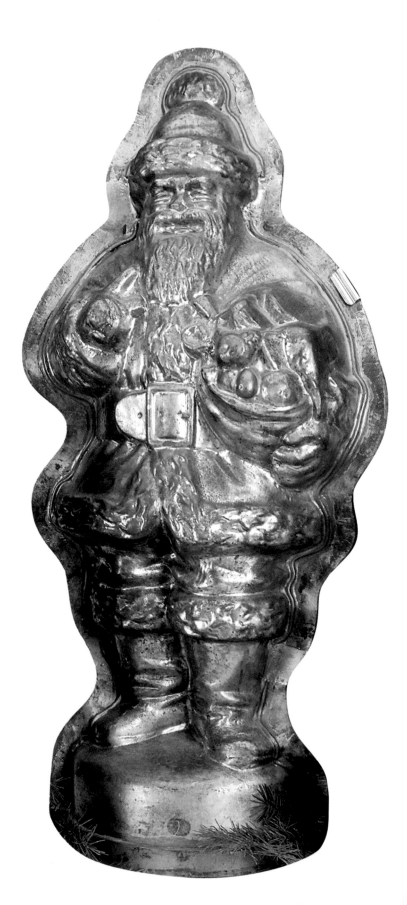

The little tableau of Christmas collectibles, far right, is arranged on a windowsill under a cone-studded wreath. It shows how pieces from different times and places can be displayed effectively together. The central figure is, of course, Santa Claus. This gnome-faced St. Nick sits on a cardboard log that once contained candy. His head is bisque and his clothes are made of crepe paper.

Sitting on the sled are two dolls with bisque heads and hands; they are dressed in their original crocheted clothes. They, too, were candy containers. The three tiny dolls on a sled are toys made by Hubach, a German toymaker. Next to them is a German bisque-headed angel with pressed paper, known as Dresden, wings. The lithographed paper sled is dated 1896 and is an American candy box. The three children with the snowball

candy boxes are made of tightly wound cotton. Their heads are bisque and they are dressed in handmade clothes. Coasting between two snowballs is a girl on a sled. Made of blown glass, as a Christmas tree ornament, this figure is so uncommon and so fragile that it is no longer hung from the tree. The little girl on skis is also a bisque and cotton Hubach toy.

The rare Santa penny toy, below left, is made of lithographed tin. It is only three and a half inches long and two and three-quarters inches tall. The lid of the sled slides open to reveal a little treat. Manufactured in Germany at the turn of the century, tiny toys like this sold for a penny each. Today, they sell for hundreds of dollars.

Board games are also popular with collectors. The one shown on the left, titled "A Visit from Santa Claus," was manufactured early in the twentieth century and traces Santa's journey on Christmas Eve.

More Collectibles

Kugels (German for ball or globe) are among the earliest glass ornaments and perhaps the most eagerly sought by collectors. Heavy glass lined with bright color, they probably originated in Lauscha, Germany, in the middle of the nineteenth century. By 1890 they had become popular in America.

Forerunners of modern blown-glass Christmas balls, the shimmering kugels were made in many shapes, sizes, and colors. There are grape clusters that vary in length from three to eleven inches and heavy glass globes from an inch or two up to fourteen

inches in diameter. There are also oval kugels and some that are ribbed "melons." The most common colors are silver, green, and gold; cobalt, turquoise, and purple are more unusual. Most highly prized are deep red kugels in any shape.

The kugels on the left are hung on the "branches" of a specially designed iron tree, which is sturdy enough to display a collection of heavy but fragile kugels. The branches are wrapped in cotton as many thrifty Pennsylvania Germans did with a real tree after its needles had dropped off. (The "cotton trees" were then stored in the attic for future Christmases.)

The sweet-faced doll on the right is another nineteenth-century ornament. Almost two feet tall, with jointed feet, she wears a cotton-batting dress trimmed with crepe paper ribbons. With her pink dress and pretty pansies, she does not look like a Christmas decoration, but at the time she was made, harps, gondolas, horseshoes, even fish and pickles were ornaments of the season.

By the end of the nineteenth century, creating ornaments at home had become an important hobby, encouraged by features in magazines like *The Youth's Companion*, *Godey's Lady's Book*, and *Ladies Home Journal*, and supplied with the wealth of embossed and lithographed paper "scraps" in stores.

Victorian Trees and Ornaments

Christmas trees made of feathers, intricately detailed "Dresdens," and ornaments made of pressed cotton are all highly prized by modern collectors. The trees on these pages were created of feathers and decorated as they might have been early in the twentieth century.

Feather trees, which originated in nineteenth-century Germany, are the first artificial Christmas trees. Made of dyed-green goose feathers, these trees could be used from year to year. They were usually small enough to put on a tabletop, like the two trees shown here, but occasionally quite large ones, up to seven feet tall, were created.

Early in the twentieth century, the feather trees began to be made in America by the Pennsylvania Germans. Charming new ones are still being produced and, like the old ones, they sell quickly.

"Dresdens" are German fancies that were made between 1880 and World War I by die-stamping imaginatively shaped gold and silver cardboard, which was then tinseled and beribboned. Originally manufactured as party favors, most Dresdens were hollow so a sweet tidbit could be hidden inside. In the interest of increased sales, however, merchants suggested to their customers that Dresdens would look wonderful on their Christmas trees. And, indeed, they did, for these lightweight decorations

were shiny and caught the light of the candles on the tree.

Many nineteenth-century ornaments were created in cottage industries with entire families participating in the process. To fashion the pressed-cotton ornaments, cotton batting was wound tightly around wire armatures in such varied shapes as people, animals, fruit, and vegetables. The finished ornaments were then embellished with paint, and sometimes a dusting of mica, and the people and animals were given composition or printed-paper faces.

The same lithographed pictures that went into Victorian scrapbooks and valentines were combined with cotton batting, tinsel, spun glass, and crepe or gilt paper to create unique contributions to the Christmas tree. Today these wonderful old "scraps," "tinsels," and "cottons" are treasured by collectors.

The antique feather tree, far left, has clip-on candle holders and is decorated with a wealth of pressed cotton, blown glass, and other three-dimensional Dresden ornaments, as well as tiny American flags, which were common trimmings on turn-of-the-century trees. A Dresden angel tops the tree.

The little feather tree left has candle holders built in the tips of the branches. It is hung with hand-colored pressed-cotton fruit and vegetables, some frosted with mica, and blown-glass ornaments. The Dresden angel has a bisque head.

Noah's Ark Toys

Many nineteenth-century Americans believed that the Bible held the solutions to all their problems, the answers to all their questions, the very code of their behavior. In addition, it was full of stories and parables that taught their children the lessons that in time would guide them through life.

These God-fearing people, who frowned on any frivolity on the Sabbath, permitted their children to play with Noah's ark toys because of their biblical background. This "Sunday toy," as it was called, wasn't banned on the Sabbath along with the other playthings, and it redeemed many a child's empty hours.

So charming were these hand-carved arks and the creatures inhabiting them that today they have become part of the annual holiday decorations.

We owe the tradition of hand-carved and hand-painted arks and their menageries to nineteenth-century Germany, where carving toys was a cottage industry that supplied a demanding market: the tiny houses, people, trees, and animals were exported to all parts of the world. The German origin of the toy ark accounts for its tall, narrow shape and brightly painted decoration; the high, pitched roofs and many windows of those early toys resemble the village houses where the carvers lived. The rare, old two-story German ark above is an excellent example. The latched sides drop open and there is a porch on the side and a hayrack in back.

The flat-topped ark left is about one hundred years old. It is unusual because of the painted animal heads along the sides (as if the animals could be seen through windows), in addition to the three-dimensional creatures.

Many old arks are now in museum collections. Occasionally, one will surface in an antique shop or at an auction and will fetch an astronomical price. Today, however, skilled carvers are creating these colorful Sunday toys in an amazing variety of materials, sizes, and styles.

TREES, TREES, AND MORE TREES

*P*eople have celebrated Christmas with decorated trees since at least the sixteenth century. Earliest known records reveal a tree in Latvia as early as 1510. Some people, however, credit Martin Luther himself with setting up the first indoor tree for his own children. The tree was said to be radiant with blazing "stars" in honor of the Christ child, the light of the world.

Without a doubt, however, the Germans are recognized as the master decorators of Christmas trees. From tabletop trees covered with edible ornaments to taller trees decked with shimmering glass and tinsel, German craftsmen are responsible for the Christmas tree's evolution.

Prince Albert of Germany carried the custom to England after his marriage to Queen Victoria and the birth of their children. Beginning in 1841 he set up in the royal palace the kind of decorated, present-laden, tabletop trees he had known as a child. Blessed with an aura of royal domestic bliss, this new custom became popular throughout England and, especially, in America.

A tree filled with tiny lights and old ornaments, like the one here, gives a room a warm glow that reflects family celebrations at Christmases gone by. The colorful glass kugels, blown-glass figures, tinseled scrap ornaments, embossed paper ornaments, and the old playthings under the tree are treasured for their connection with the past.

Homemade Decorations

In America before 1880, most Christmas trees were completely home-decorated with imagination, available materials, and, perhaps, the addition of some store-bought hard candies. Graceful garlands of corn, popped on the fireplace hearth or over the open flames of a wood-burning pot-belly stove, festooned the trees, sometimes alternating with strings of cranberries. Garlands of holly berries and crabapples, gilded nuts, dried fruit and flowers, and bay leaves were also used to ornament a green tree, whose simplicity was winning. It is neither difficult nor expensive to recreate these traditional trees today.

The tree far left is an excellent example. Bright red ribbons tied around bunches of dried apple rings, bundles of cinnamon sticks, gingerbread hearts, and little candles create a tree full of color and delicious scents. (To make the apple rings, use unpeeled, but cored, red apples. Thinly slice the apples horizontally. Spread the apple slices on cookie sheets and dry them in a 200-degree oven for several hours, or until the rings have dehydrated. Turn off the oven, but do not remove the dried apples until the oven has cooled.)

The tree shown top left is more sophisticated, but no less charming. Using floral wire, lemons and limes are hung on the strong branches of this small blue spruce. The fruit adds color to the tree and fragrance to the room. Bows tied with little pieces of saved ribbon, sprigs of baby's breath, and flat, fragrant, dried yarrow flowers soften the tree with airy, pretty decorations all found at home. (A balled tree like this one can be kept in a large wash basket draped with a piece of homespun cloth for an old-fashioned look and a new tree that can be planted outside after the holidays.)

The tree at the left combines several traditions. In addition to cookies and hanging candies—treats for the children and guests—early nineteenth-century trees were also decorated with little handwoven baskets filled with sweets. This was an adaptation of the German tradition of gift-giving, which often involved putting gifts in baskets made of rye straw and lined with homespun cloth. The baskets on this tree are filled with small gifts as well as candies.

Tabletop Christmas Trees

In the middle of the nineteenth century, Charles Dickens wrote about a Christmas tree, perhaps the first one he had ever seen. "I have been looking at a merry company of children assembled round that pretty German toy, a Christmas tree. The tree was planted in the middle of a great round table and towered high above their heads. It was brilliantly lighted by a multitude of little tapers; and everywhere sparkled and glittered with bright objects."

The Christmas tree that Prince Albert introduced to England was such a tree. It stood on a table, but in addition to the small gifts with which it was decorated a profusion of presents was artfully arranged around it.

Tabletop trees, like the one shown at the bottom right, allow the use of a living tree. This tree is potted in an earthenware crock. Displayed on a table, it is decorated with paper Santas, strings of fresh cranberries, and candy canes. A Santa Claus candy mold has the place of honor at the top of the tree.

The tabletop tree on the far right is a "family tree" and is trimmed the same way every year, with iced gingerbread cookies cut out in the shapes of hearts, stars, people, and the children's hands, with their names written in icing. Red bows, tiny lights, and old-fashioned candles (just for show) complete the decoration. The tree has been planted for the holidays in a wooden box.

The whimsical little tree planted in the small pottery bowl, top right, is displayed not on a table, but on the mantel. It is decorated with baby's breath, tiny fresh pine cones (attached with floral wire), and spritely pink-and-white-checked gingham bows.

Unusual Trees

Some of the most memorable and charming Christmas trees are those that are in some way unusual. The tree on the left is an excellent example. It is decorated with silvery lunaria (often called "honesty"), rose hips, dried apple slices, and bay leaves, which are attached to the branches with floral wire. Flowing bows of natural-colored raffia are tied to the tips of branches. The sunflower that tops the tree is glued to a cardboard cone that fits over the top branch. The flower's petals are made of large dried bay leaves. The center is simply half a small pomegranate. A rope of dried pomegranates and bay leaves follows the curve of the curtains.

The tree above is not a proper tree at all. It is a bare branch from which many smaller branches grew. Gingerbread cookies hang from the branches and recall an old Pennsylvania German custom. The branch is set into a log, around which are arranged tiny farm animals and figures within a miniature picket fence. This tabletop "tree" would make a fine folk art centerpiece for a buffet table.

Trees All Through the House

During the holidays there really is not a room in the house where a decorated tree will not add a festive touch. In the master bedroom, below, for example, the tree in the corner is decorated with dried flowers. The dummy-board Santa, who appears to have just come down the chimney, provides additional Christmas spirit.

On an old butter table, with a crank to press the moisture out of the butter, in the kitchen of an early eighteenth-century New England house, right, a small tree is planted in a basket and decorated with gingerbread cookies and small cooking utensils.

In some homes every room is decked out from early December until Twelfth Night. Even the children have their own Christmas trees in their rooms.

Fragrant Tree Ornaments

The tree on the right is in the keeping room, a multipurpose family room that runs the width of an eighteenth-century center-chimney house. The focus of the room is a large fireplace. The tree is surrounded with baskets that will be filled with gifts on Christmas morning. The fruit in the centerpiece on the table has been arranged in a pretty birdbath. The tree is trimmed with ribbon bows, a collection of charming small decorations, and fragrant ornaments made from a delicious-smelling paste of applesauce and cinnamon.

To make these ornaments you will need eight ounces of powdered cinnamon and a one-pound jar of applesauce. One week before you plan to trim the tree, and starting with small amounts, mix the cinnamon and applesauce, adding one, then the other, until the mixture reaches a cookie-dough consistency. (Too much applesauce and the mixture will be too sticky; add cinnamon. Too much cinnamon and it will be too dry; add more applesauce.) Take a lump of the paste the size of an orange and flatten it with your hands to a thickness of ¼ inch. Cut with cookie cutters and then, using a toothpick, make a hole for hanging near the top of each one. Place the ornaments on cookie sheets lined with waxed paper. Put them in a warm place to dry for one week, turning the ornaments every day.

Candlelit Christmas Trees

The tradition of the illuminated Christmas tree is recorded as early as the seventeenth century in Germany. Wax was expensive, so wicks suspended in nutshells filled with oil were substituted. In 1867, an American invented the counterweight candleholder using unfired clay balls to balance the weight of the candles and hold them in place. German ornament makers quickly adapted the counterweight holders, casting lead pine cones and stars to balance the candles. These weighted holders, however, limited candles to the very strongest branches. Clip-on candleholders, invented later, were lightweight and secure. Many of the clip varieties have crimped tin disks at the base to catch dripping wax.

It is dangerous to use candles on trees. Carefully positioned on a very fresh tree with nothing too close over the wicks, especially paper and wax ornaments and other branches, and a fire extinguisher close by, a tree can be illuminated with the special light from candles for a little while. People should always be present, however,

and many candle snuffers should be close at hand. A far easier alternative is to put ornamental candles on the tree, but use small electric lights for illumination.

All the trees on these pages are illuminated with candles and trimmed with ornaments that are relatively fire-proof. The holly tree top left reflects a practice of decorating whole holly trees, which predates European and American tree farms of the late nine-teenth century. As roads improved, pines and spruces were brought into town just before Christmas and sold in tree markets. This holly tree was grow-ing in an out-of-the-way place. With its shiny leaves and berries, it is a stunning choice for nonflammable pewter orna-ments and candles.

The tree far left is trimmed with hand-blown glass ornaments. The insides of the decorations are "sil-vered" by injecting a silver nitrate solution into each ornament and coat-ing the inside with a swirl. Later the ornaments are individually decorated with lacquer-based paint.

The tree on the left is decorated with dried, flat, densely colored yarrow flow-ers, homemade ornaments of needle-point and counted-thread embroidery, and carefully spaced yellow candles.

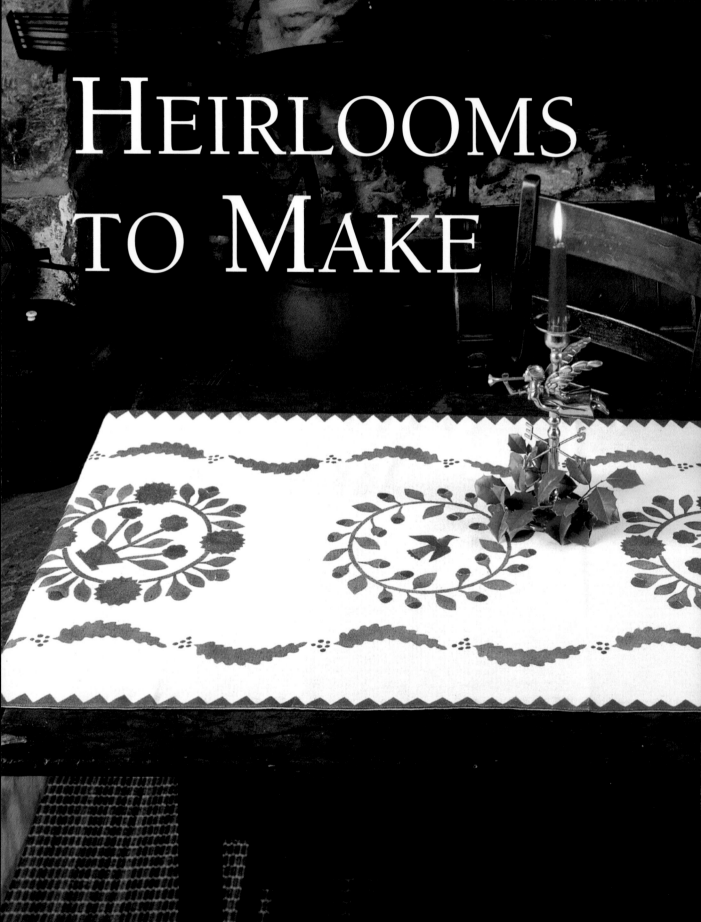

HEIRLOOMS TO MAKE

andmade is always special, particularly if there is tradition behind it. Add to that the uncommon pleasure and anticipation of using something made just for the season, a certain decoration or table linens made in the style, even the techniques, of long ago, and you have the very definition of heirloom: a valuable or interesting possession handed down from generation to generation.

All of the projects selected here have generations of American crafts traditions behind them. There is an appealing, elfin Santa holding a tiny wooden box decorated—by you—in the same manner as the landscape-painted walls in early New England homes. A dummy board, or "silent companion" is a nearly life-size image with eighteenth-century Dutch and English origins. The angel is quintessentially early American; she is fashioned of that most American of materials, corn-husks. Endearing little creatures made of seed pods and nutshells recall not only their woodland origins but their direct connection to the handmade objects of the past.

In your hands, they link you to a tradition of making the simplest of decorations by hand and sharing in the creativity of transforming raw materials, scraps, even found objects, into cherished ones.

A Holiday Table Runner to Stencil

The appliquéd squares of Baltimore Album Quilts were traditionally made in the holiday colors of bright reds and greens and they have a marvelous festive look. These lovely designs have been adapted so they may be stenciled on a table runner for a dining room table. Preparing the stencils and measuring and marking the fabric will take a bit of patience and concentration. The stenciling itself, however, can be done in half a day, even by a beginner.

Instructions

Prewash the fabric to remove the starch. Cut the runner to 24 x 72 inches, plus an extra inch on all sides for the hem. Cut each napkin to an 11-inch square, to be hemmed to a 9-inch square. Iron the runner and the napkins.

Enlarge the designs proportionately by the photocopying method. The sawtooth design should measure 1 inch high.

Wreaths: Divide the green part of the design onto two stencils as shown in the illustrations. Make a third stencil for the red shapes. Draw register marks and guidelines on the stencils.

Holly Leaf Border: Divide the green part of the design onto one stencil and the red part onto a second stencil. Draw register marks and guidelines.

Corner Flower: Divide the green part of design onto one stencil and the red part of the design onto a second stencil. Draw register marks and guidelines.

Sawtooth Border: Trace design onto one stencil. Draw register marks and guidelines.

Cut out the stencils.

Stencil paper proofs of all the designs, making two each of the wreaths.

Tape the fabric smoothly to a firm surface, stretching it out to eliminate any wrinkles.

Mark off with pins where the borders will go. Use the diagram to place the designs correctly. Place the sawtooth border directly against the outside edge of the runner. The holly leaf border begins 3 inches from the outside edge and measures 3 inches high. The corner flower measures 3 inches square and is stenciled at each corner of the holly leaf border.

Make a line of pins down the center of fabric. Space the wreaths evenly along this line.

Using the paper proofs, place all your designs and check their spacing.

Stencil all the designs, removing the pins as you place the stencils.

Stencil a corner flower on each napkin.

When the fabric paint is dry, heat seal it using a hot iron to bond the paint to the fibers.

The runner may be hem stitched by hand or lined with a lighter muslin. Hem stitch the napkins.

Materials

26 x 74-inch (unhemmed) piece of heavy weight unbleached muslin or a similar homespun-type fabric.

Additional fabric for napkins

Fabric paint, red and green

2 large stencil brushes

Stencil material (acetate or Mylar)

You Will Also Need:

Utility knife for cutting stencils

Felt-tip indelible marking pen with fine tip (to trace designs and draw register marks and guidelines)

Piece of glass (to cut stencils on)

Yardstick

Old tray

Masking tape

Old terrycloth towel and washcloth, moistened (to wipe surplus paint from brush and to keep fingers free of paint)

Ironing board and iron

Straight pins (for marking fabric)

Allow 1" hem   Bird Wreath   Flower Wreath   Holly Leaf Border   Sawtooth Border   Corner Flower

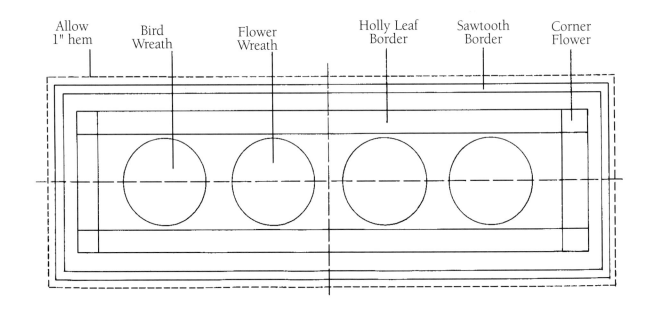

Holly Leaf Border:

Green

Red

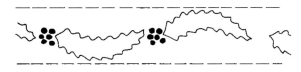

Corner Flower:

Green

Red

Sawtooth Border:

Bird Wreath:

Flower Wreath:

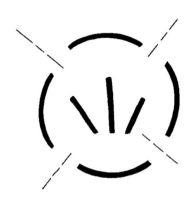

Belsnickel Dummy Board

Painted, cut-out figures, also known as dummy boards or silent companions, probably originated in the Low Countries, an aspect of the Netherlandish delight in illusionistic effects. They were also found in England during the seventeenth and eighteenth centuries. Children, servants, and pets were the most frequently depicted subjects, and the boards were placed in corridors or dark corners to suggest a friendly presence.

This impressive Christmas dummy board depicts *Der Belsnickel*, a character in the German Christmas pantheon. *Der Belsnickel* was one of Santa's assistants and is usually portrayed wearing a long coat with a hood and a pocket or pouch filled with apples. Bearing a gift of apples is symbolic of an Old World custom celebrating Adam and Eve Day on the day before Christmas. The Belsnickel carries a fistful of switches as a warning to naughty children, but he also carries a fir tree as a gift to reward the good ones.

Materials

Sheet of ¾-inch cabinet-grade finished plywood *or* sheet of ½-inch Bienfang foamboard
#220 and #400 grit sandpaper
Brown paper bag
Paper towels
Gesso
Tracing paper to fit pattern
#2 pencil
Craft knife
Disposable palette paper for acrylic paints
Small sea sponge
Clear shellac
Right Step Matte Acrylic Varnish
Krylon Matte Spray Finish #1311
Winsor & Newton Liquin Oil Painting Medium
Burnt Umber oil paint (for "antiquing" process only)
Brass hinge

Palette (Delta Ceramcoat Acrylic Colors *or* equivalent):
Fleshtone #2019
Tomato Spice #2098
Adobe Red #2046
Black #2506
Christmas Green #2068
White #2505
Hammered Iron #2094
Burnt Umber #2025
Wedgwood Blue #2069
Burnt Sienna #2030
Candybar #2407

Black Green #2116
Golden Brown #2054

Brushes:
Bette Bird Series 400 #0 Liner
Winsor & Newton Series 500 #4
    and #8 Bright
Winsor & Newton Series 520 #2
    and #4 Round
Winsor & Newton Series 995 ¾-inch
    Flat Watercolor (Wash)
Robert Simmons Fabric Master Series
    RS4331F #4 and #8 Flat Scrubber
Several l-inch and 2-inch disposable
    polyfoam brushes

Instructions
Enlarge the pattern on pages 84 and 85 to a height of 34 inches onto tracing paper. Use the grid system or enlarge mechanically by photocopying. Cut out the shape of the Belsnickel and trace this outline onto plywood or foamboard.

To transfer the pattern to the board, lightly rub a #2 pencil on the back of the tracing paper over the pattern lines. With a paper towel, lightly wipe away any loose graphite dust. Place the pattern on the board with the pencil-shaded side facing down and retrace those pattern lines which indicate changes in base coat color.

If you are using plywood, cut out the shape with a saw. Seal front, back, and edges of the wooden cutout with clear shellac and let dry. Then lightly sand all surfaces with #400 sandpaper. Apply several coats of gesso all around the cut edges of the board. (This will eliminate the layered look of plywood.)

Basic Painting Techniques
It will take two or three light base coats of most colors to obtain even coverage. Heavy coats of paint will only create ridges. Always be sure one coat of paint is completely dry before painting the next coat. Using a piece of brown paper bag, lightly smooth the final coat.

With acrylic paints, the most effective method of shading and highlighting is to float on a wash of color with a side-loaded Bright brush. To accomplish this, first wet the brush and blot the excess water onto a paper towel. Next, dip one corner of the wet brush into the paint and press the brush out wide to move the paint across the bristles while gradually stroking the brush a short way on the palette paper. The color should gradually blend out across the brush from paint to clear water.

Place the paint-filled edge of the brush against the detail shadow line traced on your board and stroke on the paint. The result should be a soft blending of color. It is usually necessary to repeat this step several times to obtain the desired depth of shading. Always allow the paint to dry between these applications of shading.

A simpler method of shading is to outline all the traced detail lines with the liner brush using the designated shadow color for that area and then dry brush or "scrub" in the shadows. For this technique, first dip a flat scrubber into the paint and rub most of the paint off on palette paper. Next, lightly scrub the color onto the board against the shadow side of your detail lines. Again,

shadows can be intensified with additional applications of paint, but always be sure to let the previous coat dry.

Face: Paint the base coat on the face using 2 or 3 coats of Fleshtone. When the final coat is dry, smooth with a piece of brown paper bag. Lightly trace on the features. Base in eyes with White paint. Use liner brush to define all other traced features with Fleshtone darkened with a little Burnt Umber. Begin floating a 1:1 mixture of Burnt Sienna and Burnt Umber around the outside of the face, on the brow wrinkles, and around the eyes and nose. Intensify shadow with several layers of floated color. Using the liner brush, darken the line work on the face with Burnt Umber. Float several layers of Adobe Red in the lower cheek area. Paint a thin layer of Adobe Red over the lip and fill in mouth area with Burnt Umber. Float thin White in the areas around the eyes, nose, cheeks, lip, and forehead that you wish to highlight.

Paint the iris of the eyes with Wedgwood Blue and add a highlight on the bottom curve with a little floated White. Paint the pupils Black. Float a shadow of Burnt Umber on each eye under the lid area. Place a dot of White on the left side of each pupil just above the center. Enhance the eyes with more Burnt Umber line work if desired.

Coat and Hood: Using Tomato Spice apply the base coat following the instructions on page 80. Brush paint out into the beard and tree areas because they will be painted on top of the clothing. Retrace in the detail lines that apply here. Mix a little Black into Candybar and float in all shadow and fold areas, repeating as many times as necessary to obtain sufficient shading.

Apples: Base-coat with one coat of Adobe Red and wash over with a thin coat of Tomato Spice. Shade around and behind the apples with Candybar mixed with a little Black. Create a crescent-shaped dimple on each apple with floated Candybar mixture. Highlight with floated White under the dimple. Add a Black stem.

Mittens: Base-coat with Christmas Green and float in shading with Black Green.

Snow, Furs, and Hair: Base-coat all areas with Hammered Iron.

Snow: Lighten Hammered Iron 1:1 with White. Pick up a small amount of paint on a half-dollar-size piece of sea sponge. Pounce the sponge lightly on the brown paper bag to distribute the paint over the sponge. Then pounce the color, using quick, springy motions, over the background area around the boots. Allow some base coat to show through as shadow. Let dry and repeat using white paint.

Fur: On the flat scrubber, pick up some of the Hammered Iron mixed with White. Swirl it on, over the background color, on the cuffs of the sleeves, pocket, front placket, and hem. Allow some of the base coat to show through as shadow. Let dry and repeat using White.

Hair: Load a #4 round brush with White paint and, starting from the bottom of the beard, begin painting rows of wavy hair-like strokes over the base coat, moving upward in layers toward the face. Using Hammered Iron, repaint moustache and add fine lines of hair around face and on the brow line with liner brush. Let dry and highlight these areas with White overstrokes.

Boots: Base-coat with Black. Let dry, then sponge a little White paint in front of toe and instep to settle the boots into the snow. Highlight some creases in the boots with floated White paint.

Fir Tree: Base-coat in Black Green. Retrace the details on the pattern to establish points of individual boughs of tree on the left side over the beard. Let dry. Using the ¾-inch wash brush, high-light the edges of the boughs in layers with floated Christmas Green. Wiggle or zigzag these rows of floated color across the tree to give them a "flame stitch" appearance.

Tree Trunk: Base-coat with Burnt Umber. Shade with Black and highlight with White.

Switches: Base-coat Black in the shadow area where switch-es extend out beyond the coat. Paint long strokes of Burnt Umber with a round brush to resemble switches. Let dry, then highlight the length of each switch with a stroke of Golden Brown.

Back and Edges of Board: Paint Black. Remember to sign and date your work.

Antiquing and Finish: Using a 2-inch polyfoam brush, apply two coats of Right Step Matte Acrylic Varnish. Allow to dry overnight.

On palette paper, mix Liquin Oil Painting Medium with Burnt Umber *oil* paint. The consistency should be light and creamy. Using a polyfoam brush, rub this glaze all over front of dummy board. Maintain a smooth, even coat.

Begin with the face and rub the glaze out fairly clean with a piece of soft paper towel. Change the paper towels frequently. Wipe out more highlight areas, leaving more glaze in the shadows.

When satisfied with this shading process, apply a light coat of Krylon Matte Spray to set the antiquing and make it feel dry to the touch. Now, using a brush, add more straight Burnt Umber oil paint in the shadow areas that really need depth and all around the perimeter of the dummy board. Soften the edges using paper towels or your fingers. Spray again lightly with Krylon Matte Spray to seal and protect the painting. Let the board dry thoroughly for several days and then finish with several coats of Right Step Matte Acrylic Varnish.

Assembly: For the *wooden* dummy board, prepare an easel support by attaching a 2 x 26 x ¾-inch board to the back side with a brass hinge so that the board can be folded flat for storage. Paint the support Black. Alternatively, screw the wooden dummy board to a 4 x 20 x ¾-inch base painted Black.

For the *foam board* dummy board, prepare an easel support by attaching a 2 x 26-inch piece of black matboard to the back side using black fabric tape. This adhesive tape will make it pos-sible to fold the board to flat for storage.

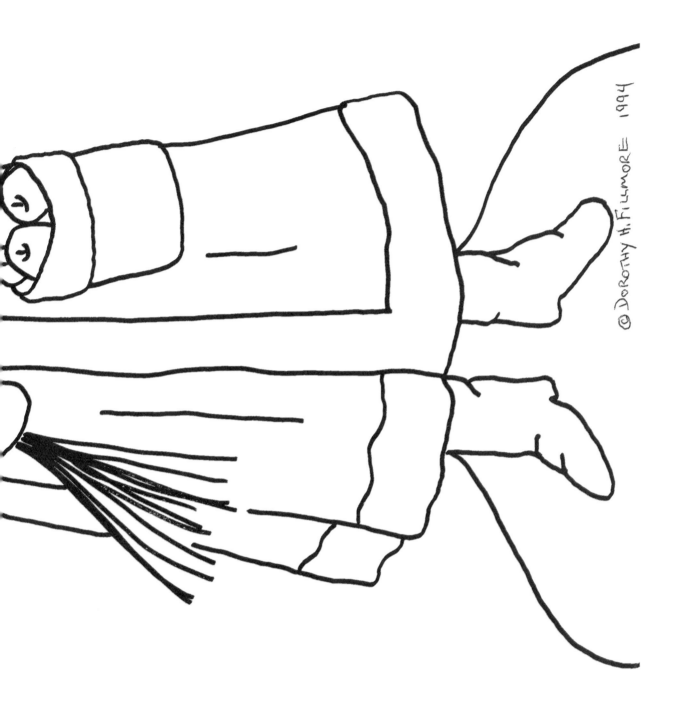

© DOROTHY H. FILLMORE 1994

Cornhusk Angel

Native Americans taught the colonists how to fashion a number of useful articles from cornhusks, but the best known today are simple dolls. These charming playthings must have kept children happy for many an hour, and several early cornhusk dolls have survived to become treasured heirlooms. This Christmas angel is really quite easy to make.

Materials
1-pound package cornhusks
Button and carpet thread
Scissors
Wire
Glue
Corn silk for hair
Balsa wood or thin pine for wings
Lace for trim

Instructions

Before you begin, soak the corn husks in warm water until they are pliable, about 10 minutes. Remove them from the water and wrap them in a towel to use as needed.

First Make the Head (Figure 1, page 88): Select two husks about 5 x 7 inches. Put one on top of the other and fold down the top 2 inches. Then fold down another 2 inches. From the right side of the folds, roll to form the head, adding husks if necessary to achieve the desired size. Place the rolled head in the center of another 5 x 7 inch husk. Pull the sides around the head, meeting at the back. Twist the husk once at the top of the head, then fold the husk down in back of the head and tie at the neck with heavy thread, holding the excess husk downward.

To Make the Arms (Figure 2): Cut an 18-inch length of wire. Fold each end back 1 inch into a small loop and twist to form the hands. Fold the center of a 1½ x 7 inch husk over one hand. Roll the husk diagonally up the arm and tie with thread about 1½ inches from the other hand loop. Cover the remaining middle section of wire with husks and secure with thread. Starting at each hand, diagonally wrap 1-inch strips of husks around the arms, overlapping with the next strip of husk until the wire is covered. Tie securely with heavy thread.

To Make the Sleeves: Place the wide end of a 5-inch husk about 1½ inches from each hand. Fold the husks around the arms until the edges meet. Tie the husks at the midpoint of the wire, halfway from each hand.

Position the center of the arms under the head and tie firmly with thread (figure 3), crisscrossing the shoulders and circling the neck.

To Make the Legs (Figures 4 and 5): Cut two 8-inch pieces of wire. Fold back 1 inch on the bottom of each piece to make the feet. Put each piece of wire in the center of a 5-inch wide husk. Roll the husk around each wire and tie with thread. Starting at each foot, diagonally wrap 1-inch strips of husks upward around the leg, overlapping with the next strip of husk until the leg is covered. Tie securely with heavy thread.

To Make the Body: Using thread, attach eight to ten husks at the back and front of the neck. Wind the thread around the neck, criss-crossing it over the shoulders and around the waist a couple of times. Tie the thread tightly at waist. Insert the legs into the body, making the angel 16 inches tall, and tie securely. Tie additional overlapping husks around the waist to form an inner skirt.

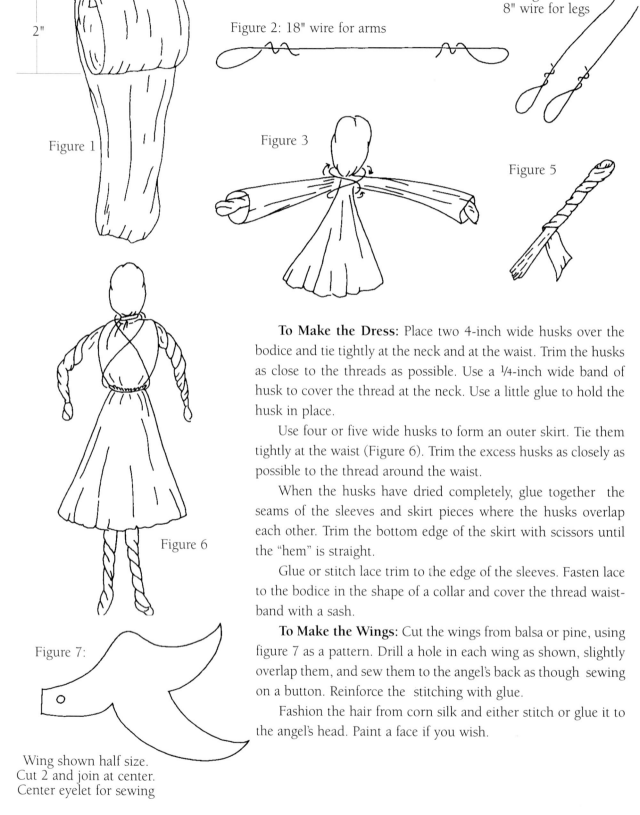

2"

Figure 1

Figure 2: 18" wire for arms

Figure 4:
8" wire for legs

Figure 3

Figure 5

Figure 6

Figure 7:

Wing shown half size.
Cut 2 and join at center.
Center eyelet for sewing

To Make the Dress: Place two 4-inch wide husks over the bodice and tie tightly at the neck and at the waist. Trim the husks as close to the threads as possible. Use a ¼-inch wide band of husk to cover the thread at the neck. Use a little glue to hold the husk in place.

Use four or five wide husks to form an outer skirt. Tie them tightly at the waist (Figure 6). Trim the excess husks as closely as possible to the thread around the waist.

When the husks have dried completely, glue together the seams of the sleeves and skirt pieces where the husks overlap each other. Trim the bottom edge of the skirt with scissors until the "hem" is straight.

Glue or stitch lace trim to the edge of the sleeves. Fasten lace to the bodice in the shape of a collar and cover the thread waistband with a sash.

To Make the Wings: Cut the wings from balsa or pine, using figure 7 as a pattern. Drill a hole in each wing as shown, slightly overlap them, and sew them to the angel's back as though sewing on a button. Reinforce the stitching with glue.

Fashion the hair from corn silk and either stitch or glue it to the angel's head. Paint a face if you wish.

A Floral Topiary

At Colonial Williamsburg, boxwood topiaries in many of the gardens help recreate the look of the eighteenth-century. In this design, dried flowers are used to achieve a handsome indoor topiary. It would look wonderful on a table in the front hall. We used a cinnamon stick for the stem, but a straight stick of similiar thickness can certainly be substituted.

Materials

Block of Oasis™ floral foam
    for dried flowers
15-inch cinnamon stick
Urn, cachepot, or flowerpot
Dried hydrangea and roses
Green sheet moss
Paring knife
Hot-glue gun

Instructions

Cut the block of floral foam in half. Using a paring knife, trim one half into a rough ball shape by cutting the corners and edges.

Trim the other piece of foam to fit into the urn, cachepot, or flower pot. Stuff the foam tightly in place.

Cut each end of the cinnamon stick to a point. Insert one end of the stick halfway through the ball like a lollipop. Remove the stick, put some hot glue into the hole, then reinsert the stick.

Insert stems of hydrangea all over the foam ball to cover it. If any stems break off, use hot glue to attach them.

Use hot glue to attach the roses.

Insert the free end of the cinnamon stick into the foam in the container. Remove the stick, put hot glue into the hole, then reinsert the stick.

Cover the foam at the base of the topiary with green sheet moss and glue on a few flowers to decorate it.

Victorian Pressed Cotton Batting Ornaments

In the late nineteenth century homemade Christmas ornaments of pressed cotton batting were very popular. Families took pleasure and pride in creating a variety of "scrap ornaments," which they saved from year to year. Since these decorations were not easily broken, they were favorites of the children. The instructions that follow are for pressed cotton batting ornaments: figures with bodies, arms, and legs made from pipe cleaners.

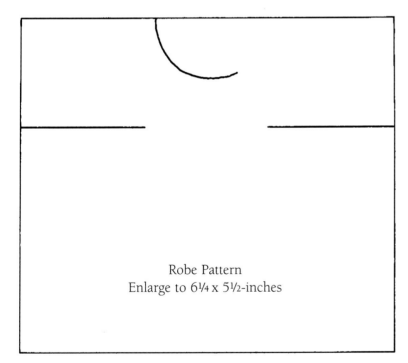

Robe Pattern
Enlarge to 6¼ x 5½-inches

Materials

Old-fashioned thin cotton batting, available at quilting supply shops

12-inch pipe cleaners

Victorian face scraps: Santas, cherubs, children, available at large craft stores

Trim: gold stars, braid, lace, beads, sequins

Thin gold cord

Cotton balls

You Will Also Need:

Scissors

Craft glue

Toothpicks

Instructions

Cut batting pieces as follows:

    Robe—see pattern

    Cape—2½ x 7 inches

    Hood—2½ x 5 inches

    Arms—2½ x 2 inches

    Legs—4 x 2 inches

    Strip around neck—¾ x 6½ inches

    Strip around waist—¾ x 4 inches

1. Fold two pipe cleaners in half, twisting them together once in the middle to form the arms and legs. Fold each arm in half and twist to secure.

2. For the head, fold a third pipe cleaner 5 inches from one end, so that approximately two-thirds of it is doubled.

3. Twist the entire length of the doubled part together. Bend the twisted part into a loop to form the head, securing it by twisting the doubled end around the top of the single part.

4. Attach the head to the body by twisting the remaining pipe cleaner below the head to the body section.

5. For the feet, fold up the bottom of each leg 1½ inches and twist to secure.

6. Using a toothpick, spread glue evenly over the length of the batting to be use for the leg. (Glue only one at a time.)

7. Wrap the batting lengthwise around the leg, twisting firmly to tighten it. Repeat for the other leg and both arms. Allow the glue to dry completely before proceeding.

8. Push a cotton ball through the loop of the head to form the face.

9. Make the hood by folding a small lip of material to the outside. Put the hood material around the head so the length falls in front of the figure. Adjust the hood in back by making small pleats, then glue in place. Secure to the front of figure with glue.

10. Carefully fit cotton batting robe around figure, adjusting with folds as needed. Overlap the front of the robe and glue in place. Run a thin line of glue along the length of the sleeve. Carefully press sleeve together around pipe cleaner.

11. Arrange the scarf strip around neck, bringing together as a V in the front at the waist and tacking with glue. Wrap belt strip around waist and glue in place. Position the arms by bending gently. For a muff, bring arms together, cut a strip of batting 1 inch wide, spread with glue, and wrap around the ends of the sleeves to secure.

12. Glue face scrap to the cotton ball. Decorate figure with trimmings, as desired. Sew thin cord to the hood for hanging.

Christmas Critters

Part of the fun of making critters is foraging for the materials they're made of. A beautiful fall day that draws you out of the house is the perfect time to set out; take a bag or a basket and put on your walking shoes. Search the roadsides for sturdy materials that keep their shape when dry—teasel, goldenrod, evening primrose, and milkweed pods, pine cones, gum tree balls, and acorns and acorn caps. Supplement your finds with dried strawflowers, gomphrena, baby's breath and the like from craft shops and florists. Crack walnuts carefully so both halves of the shell are usable. Black-eyed peas make eyes. Rose hips are buttons or filling for an acorn-cap basket. Create birds from milkweed pods and save their white silk for fur for another critter. Dried okra pods, bracket fungus you find on tree trunks, slices of corn cob, and the stems of broom corn with the kernels still attached give you opportunities to invent entirely new species. Give your imagination free rein.

Before you start, bake pine cones, pods, and other suspect material in a 200-degree oven for about 25 minutes, or microwave 2 to 5 minutes on high to kill any insects, larvae, or eggs that might be there.

Hot glue makes assembling critters easy and quick. (Be careful of your fingers; practice if you've never used a glue gun before.) Glue a small horizontal teasel (for a head) near the large end of a large horizontal teasel (the body). Push a scrap of a pine cone scale into the small end of the head teasel for a beak. Add a few strands of milkweed silk to the back of the large teasel for feathers, and add pine cone scales under the body for feet, and you've got a duck. Whole pine cones also make good bodies. Milkweed pods split lengthwise make wings. Twisted okra pods are curly tails, acorns are heads, corn silk is hair, pine cone scales are just right for ears, feet, or beaks, as are acorns, pumpkin seeds, and berries for eyes and dried leaves for ears. Critters hold dried grass or flowers in their paws and take naturally to a flower tucked behind an ear, around their neck, or on top of an acorn-cap hat.

An Heirloom Santa

This whimsical little Santa Claus is not difficult to make, and he is small enough to fit on a narrow shelf. The box he holds can be heaped with tiny candies instead of the pine cones, berries, and tiny pine boughs shown here. This is the kind of decoration that is treasured more and more as the years pass.

Materials

¼ yard bleached muslin or a lightweight cotton fabric

3½ x 2½-inch oval wooden
plaque (cut out yourself or
purchase from a craft store)

Polyester stuffing

1¾ x 1¼ x ⅛-inch piece of
balsa wood for the lid of the box

3¼ x 1¾ x 1¼-inches piece of
balsa wood for the box

2 fingertips, each 1¾ inches long,
cut from old leather gloves, or
use black felt to make mittens

Glue or small brads

Gesso

Acrylic paint in the following colors:
white, black, brown, sienna,
Indian red, yellow, naphthol
red light, green

Tiny pine cones, berries,
tiny boughs of pine, to be glued
in the box

Satin-finish polyurethane varnish

Instructions

Photocopy the patterns on pages 98 and 99 onto heavy paper. Cut out the patterns.

Using the patterns, cut out two pieces of muslin for the body shape, one piece for the base, and four pieces for the ears. Allow ½ inch all around on all the pieces for seams.

Sew the back and front body pieces together. Turn so the right side is out.

Sew the fabric base to the body. Begin at the sides, then the front; ease to fit. Leave part of the back open.

Stuff the body with the polyester. Stitch the opening closed by hand.

Sew the two pieces of each ear together. Trim the seam to ¼ inch, turn right side out, and stitch to the body, following the pattern for placement.

Attach Santa to the wooden base by gluing or tacking the edge of the base fabric to it.

Apply a thin coat of gesso to the entire Santa figure. Be sure to cover the tacks around the base and the stitches of the ears and the back of the ears. Set aside to dry. If more coverage is necessary, apply a second coat of gesso. When the gesso is completely dry being painting.

Paint coat and hat with a mixture of Indian red and naphthol red light. Paint the face a pale flesh color with white tinted with naphthol red light. Beard is white with gray shadows (white mixed with black).

Details of face: Eyebrows and mustache are white, eyes are black, outlines of nose and ears are brown, shading around nose is naphthol red light. Add tiny white dots at end of the nose to give dimension.

Fur around hat, collar, and bottom edge of hem is black with many overstrokes of black, yellow and white.

Paint coat and arm details in black. Pants and shoes are black with gray details (white mixed with black.)

Set aside to dry.

Glue pieces of balsa wood together to make the box.

Do not attach the lid to the box yet.

Paint the inside and the outside of the box antique white (mix white paint with a tiny bit of brown). Set aside to dry.

Freehand paint, sponge paint, or stencil the box.

When the paint on the Santa and the box are thoroughly dry, varnish with satin-finish polyurethane.

To assemble: Lay Santa flat. Apply glue to the back of the box and attach to Santa following the pattern. Make sure the box is straight. Tuck cut ends of glove fingers behind the box and glue the tips to the side of the box. Glue the lid of the box to Santa and to the back edge of the box.

When the glue has set, stand Santa on his base and glue tiny cones, greens, and berries to look as though they are piled in the box.

Ear: Cut 4

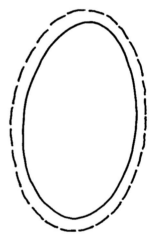

Fabric base: Cut 1

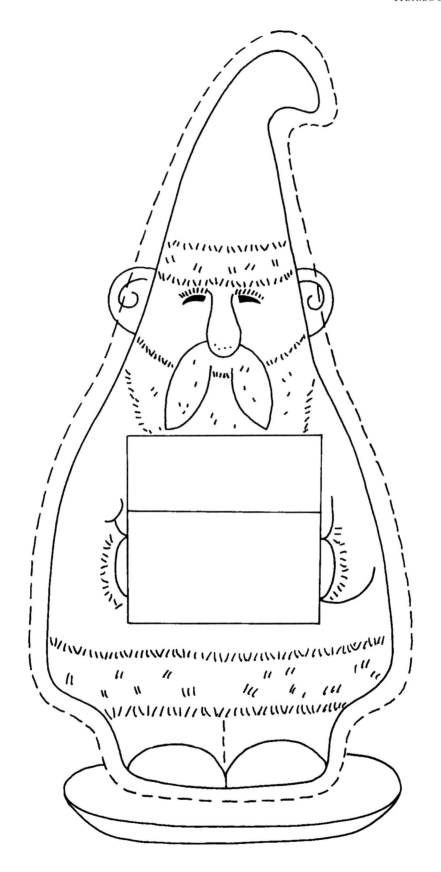

FOOD FOR
CELEBRATING

*F*ood is a Christmas companion. The Cratchits' meager Christmas dinner was festive nonetheless; the treat of an orange in the toe of a childhood stocking stays in the memory of the most well-fed adult. From a tiny gingerbread boy hung from a tree to the groaning board of English tradition, the tastes of the season are among its memorable satisfactions.

No less satisfying are the opportunities for the creative cook, whether you are one all year long, or just once a year. Here we offer meals for both kinds of cooks: memorable dishes and menus to follow to the letter or to pick and choose among.

The meals come from an American heritage that ranges all over the culinary landscape, from a seafood mousse to impress guests at a dinner party to the baked beans that accompany a hearthside supper, from simple bread and tarts to a complex hazelnut génoise. The knockout French creation of Buche de Noel, the chocolate Yule Log, is as creative as it is delicious. Joe Froggers, on the other hand, are Downeast Maine molasses cookies. Try some of our recipes; add some of your own. The most appreciated recipes of all will be those from your kitchen.

New England Holiday Dinner for Eight

The main course of this New England holiday dinner is Roast Cornish Game Hens with Orange Glaze, a nice change from the usual turkey. The fruitcake is unusual, too; it is made with cranberries and is lighter than fruitcake ordinarily is. It is not a difficult meal to prepare, since many of the dishes can be made in advance.

MENU

Mussels Steamed in White Wine
Double Squash Cream Soup
Herb Bread
Sole Mousse with Smoked Salmon
Roast Cornish Game Hens
with Orange Glaze

Pear Sorbet
Gingerbread Cookies
Fresh Cranberry Fruitcake

MUSSELS STEAMED IN WHITE WINE

This dish is delicious hot or cold and is a wonderful addition to a buffet table.

4 pounds fresh mussels
2 tablespoons butter
1 large onion, chopped
3 cups white wine (Vermouth works well)
3 bay leaves
2 tablespoons pickling spice
2 tablespoons chopped fresh parsley
1 small jar roasted pimentos, chopped

TO SERVE COLD
Leaf lettuce
1 pound cherry tomatoes
1½ cups mayonnaise
1 teaspoon curry powder
Salt to taste

Scrub and debeard the mussels. Put them into a colander and rinse them under cold running water.

In a large skillet, melt the butter. Add the onion and cook, stirring constantly, until the onion is soft and translucent. Stir in the white wine, bay leaves, pickling spice, and parsley. Bring to a boil. Add as many mussels as will fit in the pan. (If the pan won't hold them all, steam them in batches.) Cover the pan and steam the mussels for 2 minutes. Remove the cover, and, using a slotted spoon, turn the mussels. Cover the pan and steam the mussels for another 2 minutes.

Using a slotted spoon, remove the mussels to a large serving bowl, discarding any that have not opened. If the mussels are to be served hot, sprinkle them with the chopped pimento. Serve immediately.

To serve the mussels cold, cook them as directed, then refrigerate the mussels for 1½ hours, or until they are well chilled.

Open the mussels, remove and discard the shell not attached to each mussel. Arrange the mussels on the half shell on a platter lined with leaf lettuce, alternating with rows of cherry tomatoes.

In a blender, combine the mayonnaise, curry powder, and salt to taste. Place a dab of the curry mayonnaise on each mussel. For a fancier touch, use a pastry tube with a star tip and decorate each mussel with a star of curry mayonnaise.

DOUBLE SQUASH CREAM SOUP

This soup should be made a day in advance to allow the flavors to blend. It may be served in individual bowls, but it is most effective when it is served in a tureen made from a blue Hubbard squash. To make the tureen, select a large, nicely shaped squash. Remove the top third (use a saw or a sturdy serrated knife; it's a tough shell) and use it for the soup recipe. Scoop out the seeds and fibers from the rest, leaving most of the inside intact. Place cut-side down in a shallow roasting pan. Add 1 inch of water. Bake the squash in a 350-degree oven until the inside is barely tender. Check to see that the shell is not darkening too much while baking; cover with foil if it is. Do not overbake or the shell will not be firm enough to hold the soup.

5 small, tender yellow squash
2 quarts chicken broth
1 clove garlic, minced
¼ teaspoon dried oregano
½ teaspoon dried chervil
¼ teaspoon salt
Top piece of blue Hubbard squash
4 tablespoons butter, softened
½ to ⅔ cup heavy cream
3 tablespoons dark molasses

Serves 8

Preheat the oven to 350 degrees.

Wash the yellow squash and cut it into 1-inch pieces. Place in a large pot with the chicken broth, garlic, oregano, chervil, and salt. Simmer until the squash is tender.

Place the Hubbard squash, skin side up, in a shallow baking pan with 1 inch of water. Bake until the flesh is tender, about 20 minutes. Scoop the flesh out of the shell and mash it well. Measure 1½ cups and set aside. (Any mashed squash that remains can be stored, covered, in the refrigerator, and reheated to serve at another meal.)

Drain the yellow squash, reserving the liquid. Place the squash in the jar of a blender. Blend on medium-high speed until the squash is smooth. Add the butter and the mashed Hubbard squash. Blend until the ingredients are well mixed. Slowly add the cream, then the molasses. The soup should be of a thick consistency, not watery; if it's too thick, however, use some of the reserved cooking liquid to thin it. Refrigerate the soup.

Remove the soup from the refrigerator about two hours before it is to be served. Just before serving, over medium-low heat, warm the soup, but do not allow it to boil. Pour the soup into the Hubbard-squash tureen and serve.

ROAST CORNISH GAME HENS WITH ORANGE GLAZE

1 Cornish game hen per serving
1 lemon
Salt and freshly ground black
    pepper to taste
Melted butter for basting

ORANGE GLAZE FOR EIGHT HENS
2 cups sugar
1 cup orange juice
1 cup water
2 tablespoons Cointreau
2 tablespoons freshly grated
    orange peel
Orange slices, cranberries, fresh
    parsley (for garnish)

Preheat the oven to 350 degrees.

Rub the game hens with half a lemon. Sprinkle them with salt and pepper inside and out. Place the hens, breast side up, on a rack in an open roasting pan. Brush them with melted butter and roast, basting occasionally with the pan drippings, until tender, 45 minutes to 1 hour.

When the hens are cooked, arrange them on a serving platter and make the orange glaze.

In a saucepan, combine the sugar, orange juice, and water. Stir until the sugar is dissolved. Bring the liquid to a boil and cook, without stirring, on medium-high heat for approximately 5 minutes, or until the mixture has thickened and is syrupy. Stir in the Cointreau and the grated orange peel. Remove the pan from the heat and immediately pour the syrup over the roasted game hens. Arrange the orange slices, cranberries, and parsley around the edge of the platter as a garnish.

SOLE MOUSSE WITH SMOKED SALMON

1½ pounds filet of sole
¾ cup vermouth
3 bay leaves
1 teaspoon pickling spice in a
    cheesecloth bag
3 large egg whites
¼ teaspoon nutmeg
Salt to taste
2 cups heavy cream
2 envelopes unflavored gelatin
½ cup mayonnaise
¼ pound smoked salmon,
    sliced thin

DECORATION
1 cucumber, sliced paper thin
1 stuffed green olive
Fresh dill weed

Put the sole into a large frying pan, add the vermouth, bay leaves, and pickling spice. Poach the sole slowly over medium-low heat for approximately 3 to 5 minutes until it flakes when tested with a fork. Reserving the poaching liquid, remove the sole with a slotted spoon and place in the blender. At slow speed, blend the sole. Add the egg whites one at a time, blending well after each addition. Add the salt and nutmeg. While the blender is running add the heavy cream. (The mixture should be semithick at this point.) Dissolve the gelatin in ¾ cup poaching liquid. Add the gelatin and mayonnaise to the mixture in the blender and blend well.

Spray a fish-shaped mold with nonstick coating. Arrange the cucumber slices along the bottom of the mold, overlapping them in a fish-scale pattern. Carefully spoon half of the mousse mixture into the mold, spreading evenly. Place a layer of smoked salmon on the mixture, then add the remaining mousse on top of the salmon. Cover the mold with plastic wrap and chill for at least 4 hours.

Unmold the mousse onto a tray lined with lettuce leaves. Add the stuffed green olive, cut in half, for eyes, and any leftover salmon for fins. Arrange the dill weed around the mousse.

HERB BREAD

2 envelopes active dry yeast
⅓ cup lukewarm water
1 cup dry oatmeal (quick-cooking)
2½ cups boiling water
2 teaspoons salt
2 tablespoons butter, softened
⅔ cup molasses
1 teaspoon ground marjoram
1½ tablespoons anise seed
2 tablespoons fresh rubbed sage
    (if unavailable, use ground)
7 cups flour

Makes 2 large or 3 small loaves

Dissolve the yeast in warm water and set aside. Place the oats in a large bowl. Add the boiling water, salt, and butter. Mix well and let stand approximately 15 to 20 minutes until the oatmeal is soft and has cooled to lukewarm. Add the molasses, marjoram, anise, sage, and the dissolved yeast. Mix well. Add the flour a cup or two

at a time and mix well. Knead until evenly mixed and the dough is elastic.

Place the dough in buttered bowl and turn it to cover the surface with butter. Cover with a towel and let rise in a warm place until doubled in size—approximately 1½ hours.

Punch down the dough and divide it for 2 large or 3 small loaves. Knead each portion for 2 minutes on a floured cloth. Coat loaf pans with nonstick coating or butter, place the dough in them, cover, and set aside to rise again.

When risen, bake at 350 degrees for 25 to 30 minutes, checking after 15 minutes to see if the loaves are browning too much—if so, cover lightly with foil. When done, remove from oven and brush tops with butter.

PEAR SORBET

1 envelope unflavored gelatin
5 tablespoons fresh lemon juice
1⅔ cups sugar
2 cups water
3 tablespoons kirsch
6 to 7 very ripe pears, preferably
    Bartlett
2 large egg whites
¼ teaspoon vanilla extract

Makes 4 cups

Soften the gelatin in the lemon juice and set aside. In a saucepan, combine the sugar and water. Mix well, then bring to the boiling point. Gently boil without stirring for 5 minutes. Remove the pan from the heat and let cool slightly. Stir in the gelatin and the kirsch and mix well. Place the pan in the freezer. Freeze the mixture for about

1½ hours, or until it is a firm mush, then scrape it into a large bowl.

Peel, core, and mash the pears. (You should have 4 cups.) Add the mashed pears, the egg whites, and the vanilla to the frozen mixture. Beat with an electric beater until the mixture is fluffy. Put the bowl into the freezer, freeze to a firm mush, then stir to prevent crystallizing.

Transfer the sorbet to a decorative mold, cover, and freeze until firm. Just before serving, unmold the sorbet onto a serving platter and decorate with pear slices (dip them in lemon juice first to prevent their turning brown). For a nice effect, use red and green Bartlett pear slices around the sorbet. Or serve the sorbet in individual portions and decorate with pear slices or red and green grapes.

FRESH CRANBERRY FRUITCAKE

6 large oranges
4 cups all-purpose flour or cake flour
1½ cups sugar
1 tablespoon baking powder
1 teaspoon baking soda
1 teaspoon salt
½ cup butter-flavored shortening
2 eggs
½ cup cream sherry
2 cups cranberries, coarsely chopped
1½ cups dark raisins
1½ cups walnuts, coarsely chopped

Serves 12

Preheat the oven to 325 degrees. Grease and flour a 12-cup ring mold.

Grate 2 tablespoons of peel from the oranges and set aside. Squeeze ½ cup of orange juice and set aside. Chop enough orange pulp to make 2 cups.

Sift together the flour, sugar, baking powder, baking soda, and salt into a large bowl. Cut in the shortening with a pastry blender until the mixture resembles coarse crumbs.

With a fork in a medium-sized bowl, beat the eggs with the sherry and orange juice until well blended. Add this mixture, the orange peel, orange pulp, chopped cranberries, raisins, and walnuts to the dry ingredients. Stir only until the flour mixture is evenly moistened.

Spoon the batter evenly into the prepared ring mold and bake 1½ hours, or until a toothpick inserted in the center comes out clean. Turn the cake out and cool on a wire rack.

A Holiday Supper

MENU

Ham in Pastry
Spiced Peaches
Finger Rolls
Cold Chicken Mousse

DESSERT PYRAMID:
Macaroons
Walnut Meringues
Gingerbread Cookies
Hermits

Butter Tarts
Fruitcake
Chocolate Rum Truffles
Roasted Almonds
Claret Punch
Tipsy Cake
Candied Peels
Muscat Raisins
Spiced Tea

The tradition of extending hospitality to friends and family during the Christmas season, from Christmas Eve to Twelfth Night, is as old as the holiday itself. We planned this holiday supper to entertain a good number of people with as little effort as possible. Everything on the buffet table can be prepared in advance of the party, some things many days before, and set out just before guests arrive.

HAM BAKED IN A PASTRY CRUST

The pastry can be made in advance and stored in the refrigerator for a week or it can be frozen. This dish may be served either hot or cold, accompanied by good mustard and spiced peaches.

3 tablespoons ham fat, rendered
1 cup chopped onion
1 cup chopped carrots
8- to 10-pound ham, skinned and trimmed of excess fat
2 cups Madeira
2 cups beef stock
1 small bunch parsley
1 bay leaf

PASTRY
½ cup butter, chilled
¼ cup vegetable shortening, chilled
6 cups all-purpose flour
1½ teaspoons salt
¼ teaspoon sugar
2 eggs, beaten
½ to ⅔ cup ice water

Preheat the oven to 325 degrees.

In a roasting pan large enough to hold the ham, melt the ham fat over low heat on top of the stove. Add the onion and carrot, and cook over moderate heat until the onion is translucent. Place the ham in the pan, pour the Madeira and the stock over it. Add the parsley and the bay leaf to the pan. Bring the liquid to a simmer.

Cover the roasting pan closely, and braise the ham in the oven for 2 to 2½ hours, or until the ham is tender. Allow the ham to cool in the liquid.

To make the pastry, in a large bowl combine the chilled butter and shortening. Add the flour, salt, and sugar and combine, using a pastry blender or two kitchen knives until the mixture resembles coarse meal.

Beat the eggs with ½ cup ice water, then add the mixture all at once to the flour mixture. Stir with a fork until well blended, adding more water if needed.

Wrap the dough tightly and store in the refrigerator until firm enough to roll out easily.

DECORATION AND FINAL BAKING
In a small bowl, beat 1 egg with 2 tablespoons of water. Drain the ham and wipe it dry. Preheat the oven to 350 degrees. Generously grease a baking sheet with butter.

Place the chilled dough on a lightly floured linen tea towel. Roll it out as thinly as possible—quite a large rectangle will be needed to enclose the ham completely. Place the ham upside down in the center of the pastry. Using the towel to lift the pastry, fold it over the ham, cutting away excess dough as it overlaps. Seal the edges of the dough with the egg mixture. Carefully lift the ham and place it right side up on the baking sheet.

Gather up all the pastry scraps and roll them out between two sheets of waxed paper. Place it in the freezer until the dough is almost frozen—this makes it easier to cut out the decorations.

When the dough is quite firm, use a small pointed knife to make decorative pastry cutouts—we used holly leaves and berries on curving stems. Brush the egg mixture over the entire surface of the ham to give it a rich color as it bakes and to hold the decorations in place. Arrange the pastry cutouts in a pleasing pattern on the ham, pressing them gently into the dough. Brush them with the egg mixture.

Bake the decorated ham until the pastry is evenly browned—about 1 hour. Watch carefully—if one area begins to brown too quickly, cover it with a small piece of aluminum foil.

COLD CHICKEN MOUSSE
This delicious cold chicken mousse can be made one or two days in advance, kept in the refrigerator in the mold, then unmolded and decorated a few hours before it is to be served.

1 tablespoon unsalted butter
½ cup chopped scallions
2 cups well-seasoned chicken broth
2 tablespoons unflavored gelatin softened in ¼ cup dry white wine or water
2 cups finely chopped, cooked chicken breasts
3 tablespoons Madeira
Salt and white pepper
⅛ teaspoon ground nutmeg
¾ cup heavy cream, chilled
½ cup finely chopped, roasted almonds
½ cup finely minced celery
1 cup mayonnaise
Tarragon leaves
Green seedless grapes

Melt the butter in a medium-sized saucepan. Add the chopped scallions and sauté gently until tender but not brown. Stir in the chicken broth. Add the gelatin mixture to the broth. Simmer and stir until the gelatin is dissolved. Mix in the chicken.

Transfer the chicken mixture to the jar of a blender and puree until smooth. Pour into a large bowl. Stir in the Madeira, then season to taste with salt, pepper, and nutmeg. Remember

that the cream, which is added later, will dilute the flavor. Cover the bowl and chill until the mixture is almost set, stirring occasionally.

Whip the cream until it holds its shape, then gently fold it into the chicken mixture, along with the chopped almonds and celery.

Pour into a lightly oiled 6-cup mold and chill until firm.

A few hours before serving, unmold the mousse onto a serving platter. Thinly coat the mousse with the mayonnaise, keeping the surface as smooth as possible. Decorate with the tarragon leaves and halved green grapes.

CHOCOLATE RUM TRUFFLES
Store these truffles in a covered container in the refrigerator. They will keep well for about a week.

8 ounces good quality semisweet chocolate
¼ cup powdered sugar, sifted
3 tablespoons unsalted butter
3 egg yolks, slightly beaten
1 tablespoon dark rum
Makes about 2 dozen
In the top of a double boiler, melt 6 ounces of the chocolate over simmering water. Stir in the sugar and butter. Add a small amount of the chocolate to the beaten egg yolks to warm them, then add to the hot chocolate mixture, stirring thoroughly. Remove from the heat and stir in the rum. Chill without stirring for at least 2 hours.

Shape the chocolate into 1-inch balls. Grate the remaining

two ounces of chocolate onto a sheet of wax paper. Roll the balls in the grated chocolate.

HERMITS

Store these spicy cookies in an airtight container with wax paper between the layers.

2/3 cup unsalted butter
1 cup dark brown sugar
2 eggs
1¾ cups flour, sifted
¼ teaspoon baking soda dissolved in 2 tablespoons sour cream
¼ teaspoon ground nutmeg
¼ teaspoon ground cloves
2 teaspoons ground cinnamon
1 cup chopped pecans
¾ cup raisins
½ cup chopped citron

GLAZE

2 tablespoons melted unsalted butter
2 tablespoons heavy cream
1 teaspoon vanilla extract
1½ cups powdered sugar

Makes 3 dozen

Generously grease a large cookie sheet with butter. Preheat the oven to 375 degrees.

In a large bowl, cream the butter and sugar together. Mix in the eggs, one at a time, then beat thoroughly. Stir in the baking soda and sour cream. Sift the flour with the ground nutmeg, cloves, and cinnamon, then stir into the butter mixture. Fold in the pecans, raisins, and citron.

Drop from a teaspoon onto the prepared cookie sheet. Bake until lightly browned, about 15 minutes.

To make the glaze, in a bowl combine the melted butter, cream, vanilla, and enough powdered sugar to give a good consistency. Brush the glaze on the cookies while they are still warm.

BUTTER TARTS

PASTRY

1¾ cups all-purpose flour
1 teaspoon salt
⅓ cup unsalted butter, chilled
⅓ cup lard or vegetable shortening, chilled
⅓ cup ice water

FILLING

1 cup brown sugar
½ cup butter
1 egg, lightly beaten
1 cup raisins
1 teaspoon vanilla extract

Makes 12 tarts

First make the pastry. Sift the flour and salt together into a chilled bowl. Using a pastry blender and working quickly, cut the butter and the lard, or shortening, into the flour until the mixture is in bits the size of peas. Do not overblend.

Stir in the ice water, 1 tablespoon at a time, until the pastry can be gathered into a ball. (All the water may not be needed.) Wrap the dough in wax paper and chill in the refrigerator.

When ready to bake the tarts, preheat the oven to 350 degrees. Lightly butter 12 small tart pans.

To make the filling, in a small pan over very low heat, melt the butter and dissolve the brown sugar, stirring frequently. Do not allow the butter to

brown. Beat in the egg and stir over low heat until the ingredients are blended. Remove the pan from the heat. Allow the mixture to cool slightly, then stir in the raisins and the vanilla.

Remove the dough from the refrigerator. Roll the dough out quite thinly, then line the prepared tart pans. Divide the filling among the shells. Bake for 25 to 30 minutes, or until the pastry is golden and the filling has set.

TIPSY CAKE

1 large sponge cake, baked in a Turk's head or ring mold
1 cup granulated sugar
1 cup water
¾ cup dark rum or brandy
Grated rind and juice of 1 lemon
1 ounce unflavored gelatin, softened in warm water
2 cups heavy cream
Blanched almonds or candied violets for decoration

12 to 15 generous servings

Place the sponge cake in a clear glass bowl or compote. Using a fork, pierce the top and sides.

In a medium-size saucepan, combine ¾ cup of the sugar with ¾ cup of water. Cook over low heat, stirring frequently, until the sugar has dissolved. Increase the heat and bring the syrup to a boil. Boil for 10 minutes. Remove the pan from the heat and set aside until the syrup cools to lukewarm. Stir ½ cup of the rum or brandy into the syrup. Then pour the syrup slowly and evenly over the cake until most of it is absorbed.

Pour ¼ cup of warm water into a bowl. Sprinkle the softened gelatin over the water. Stir until the gelatin has melted. Stir in the remaining ¼ cup of sugar, the lemon rind and juice, and the remaining ¼ cup of rum or brandy.

In a large bowl, whip the cream until it holds soft peaks. Fold in the gelatin mixture and blend thoroughly. Spoon the cream into the center of the cake, molding it into high peaks. Any remaining cream can be spread around the base of the cake or served separately.

Store the cake, covered, in the refrigerator. Decorate with the almonds or candied violets just before serving.

MACAROONS

These macaroons can be made several days before serving and stored in an airtight container.

½ pound almond paste
1 cup granulated sugar
3 egg whites
¼ cup powdered sugar
2 tablespoons cake flour
Pinch salt

Makes about 30

Cover 2 cookie sheets with brown paper.

Crumble the almond paste into a large bowl. Gradually add the sugar and egg whites, mixing thoroughly with your hands. When all the sugar and egg white have been added and the mixture is smooth, sift in the powdered sugar, cake flour, and salt. Blend thoroughly.

Place teaspoons of the macaroon mixture onto the paper-lined cookie sheets. Flatten them slightly with fingers dipped in water. Cover and set aside for 2 hours

Preheat the oven to 300 degrees.

Bake the macaroons for 30 minutes, or until they are light brown and dry to the touch. Place the paper sheets on a towel wrung out in cold water. Carefully remove the macaroons.

WALNUT MERINGUES

Meringues are not difficult to make, but they are tricky. If the oven is too hot, or the day too humid, they will be chewy rather than crumbly, but the taste will not be affected.

2 egg whites, at room temperature
½ cup sugar
1 teaspoon vanilla extract
½ cup finely chopped walnuts

Makes about 18

Cover a cookie sheet with unglazed paper (a brown paper bag will serve). Preheat the oven to 250 degrees.

In a large bowl, beat the egg whites until they are very stiff, then beat in the sugar, 1 tablespoon at a time. Gently fold in the vanilla, then the chopped walnuts.

Using a pastry bag with a plain tube, or two spoons, arrange the meringue in small rounds on the prepared cookie sheet. Bake about 50 minutes (if meringues begin to brown, reduce oven heat), or until the meringues are dry and firm.

Remove from the paper—if they stick, wipe the back of the paper with a damp cloth.

Christmas Réveillon

The height of anticipation on Christmas Eve is perhaps best celebrated by the French, who serve a Réveillon, a grand feast after Midnight Mass. Several courses are presented with lavish preparation; the French are known for their ornamentation of food, which seems even more appropriate with the festive decorations of Christmas. Typically, a turkey with pork sausage stuffing will be the main course of the meal, which begins with tiny hors d'oeuvres and concludes with a chocolate hazelnut torte.

The tradition of the grand Christmas Eve meal in America is traced to the seventeenth century when a French-American cooking style was adapted by the Ursuline Sisters of Quebec. They combined Normandy dishes that they remembered with indigenous ingredients. As French settlers moved south into New England, the available staples and delicacies again altered, but the idea of the family feast only inspired cooks to continue to create Gallic specialties with whatever ingredients they could combine. Today, the Americanized version of a special Christmas Eve meal is no less a tradition than the French menu of the Réveillon.

Although few wait until after midnight to begin, the meal can last until the first glow of Christmas dawn. Stuffed artichokes, cheese tartlets, and other canapes are passed with glasses of wine before the guests move to the table for an appetizer of fish terrine. The main course includes roast turkey and chestnuts, white sausage, and vegetables usually arranged symmetrically with an eye to balancing color as well as the sizes and proportions of the serving platters. An elaborate display of fruits and vegetables, nuts, and flowers can center a table along with candelabra and greens. The final course at this heavily laden table includes cakes, poached pears, brandied fruits, nuts, and cheeses.

MENU

Little Deviled Eggs
Cheese Tartlets
Stuffed Mushroom Caps
Stuffed Cherry Tomatoes
Salmon Breads
Artichoke and Cheese Wreaths
Fish Terrine

Roast Turkey
with Pork Sausage and
Cornbread Stuffing
and Chestnuts
Boudin Blanc
Caramelized Apples
Carrots au Beurre

Pears in Orange Juice
Frandises aux Amandes
Chocolate Hazelnut Cake
Savarin

LITTLE DEVILED EGGS

2 dozen very small chicken eggs
Mayonnaise
Yellow mustard
Tabasco sauce or onion juice
Salt and pepper
Black olives

Makes 4 dozen

Hard boil the eggs. Cut them the long way so the yolk is cut round. Slice a small piece off the bottom of the white halves so they will stand straight. Mash the yolks with mayonnaise and mustard to a thick paste. Add Tabasco sauce or onion juice, salt and pepper to taste. Refill the whites and decorate with pieces of black olives. Refrigerate until ready to serve.

CHEESE TARTLETS

1 loaf thin-sliced sandwich bread
6 tablespoons butter, melted
½ cup mayonnaise
⅓ cup grated Parmesan cheese
1 cup grated Swiss cheese
⅓ cup chopped onion
¼ teaspoon Worcestershire sauce
2 drops Tabasco sauce
Paprika

Makes 32

Preheat oven to 400 degrees. Flatten slices of bread with a rolling pin and use a 2½-inch cookie cutter to cut rounds. Lightly brush each side with melted butter. Press into 1½-inch miniature muffin cups. Bake 10 minutes or until golden brown. Remove from oven and cool in pans. Mix mayonnaise, cheeses, onion, and Worcestershire and Tabasco sauces together. Fill each shell with mixture and

sprinkle with paprika. Place under broiler until golden and bubbly. Remove from pans. Serve immediately or cool and freeze. To serve, reheat in a 450-degree oven 7 to 10 minutes until hot.

STUFFED MUSHROOM CAPS

24 beautiful medium mushrooms
1 cup soft yellow cheese
12 thin slices of ham

Makes 2 dozen

Carefully remove the stems from the mushrooms and use a soft brush to clean. (Don't wash under water or caps will turn brown.) With a knife, cut circles in ham slightly larger than outer circumference of the mushroom. Cut a cross-hatch in the center of the ham so it will fit into the cap; place on mushroom and fill with cheese using a pastry bag with a wide tip. Refrigerate until ready to serve.

STUFFED CHERRY TOMATOES

24 firm cherry tomatoes
6 ounces cream cheese at room
*   temperature*
½ teaspoon basil
Dash of salt

Makes 2 dozen

Use a sharp knife and core the cherry tomatoes. Mix cheese, basil, and salt together and with a pastry bag, pipe cheese mixture into tomatoes. Garnish each with a tiny sprig of parsley. Refrigerate until ready to serve.

SALMON BREADS

24 slices of dark pumpernickel
*   bread*
¼ pound of smoked salmon
Sour cream
Capers

Makes 2 dozen

Cut bread with a cookie cutter in a simple shape like a crescent or circle. Cut salmon into pieces to fit bread. Use a touch of sour cream to hold salmon on the bread and add a dot on top with a caper to garnish. Refrigerate until ready to serve.

ARTICHOKE AND CHEESE WREATHS

Pimentos
12 artichoke bottoms, canned
3 ounces cream cheese
2 tablespoons sour cream or yogurt
1 teaspoon lemon juice
fresh parsley

Makes 12

Place 12 strips of pimento on wax paper and put them in the freezer. Rinse and drain artichokes. Mix together cream cheese, sour cream, lemon juice, and seasonings. Spread mixture onto the artichokes with a knife. Clip tiny sprigs of parsley and arrange in a wreath around the artichoke. Take frozen pimento and slice very thin while frozen. As the pimento thaws, it will become pliable enough to tie into bows. Press bows into cheese. Refrigerate until ready to serve.

FISH TERRINE

A food processor is needed to purée seafood in this recipe.

1 10-ounce package frozen, chopped spinach
4 scallions
2 tablespoons butter
1/4 pound fresh cooked shrimp
1/4 cup tomato paste
1 1/2 pounds fresh fillet of sole or flounder
1/2 pound fresh scallops, washed and drained
2 large eggs
2 teaspoons salt
2 cups fresh white bread crumbs
2-3 cups heavy cream
4 tablespoons lemon juice
Freshly grated white pepper
Pinch of nutmeg

Preheat oven to 350 degrees and place a roasting pan half full of water in it. Cut a piece of wax paper a little larger all around than the terrine, and a piece of aluminum foil slightly larger than that. Butter one side of the wax paper. Chop the scallions and sauté in 2 tablespoons butter with thawed, drained spinach for a minute or two. Set aside. Cut fish fillets into 2-inch pieces and purée with scallops, using a steel blade. Without turning off food processor, add eggs, salt, bread crumbs, 2 cups cream, lemon juice, several grinds of pepper, and nutmeg. Purée for 30 seconds. Mousse should hold its shape when spooned up. Add more cream if necessary. Spread a layer of fish mousse in the terrine, filling it 1/4 full. Stir a spoonful of mousse into the spinach and spread the mixture over the fish in the terrine. Cover with another layer of fish mousse. Remove all but a large dollop of mousse from the food processor. Place shrimp and tomato paste in the food processor and purée until smooth. Spread shrimp in the terrine and top with a final layer of fish mousse. Cover with wax paper, buttered side down, then foil. Set the terrine in the oven in the pan of hot water. Don't let paper or foil touch water or water may seep into the terrine. Bake 1 1/4 to 1 1/2 hours. When mousse starts to rise above rim of terrine it is almost done. An interior temperature reading of 160 degrees ensures that terrine is done, and the top will feel springy. To serve hot, leave in pan of water in oven with heat turned off and door ajar until serving time. Cut slices from terrine and serve with sour cream sauce (recipe follows), melted butter, or hollandaise sauce. To serve cold, remove mousse from oven and let cool. Drain off accumulated juices; reserve for sauce; cover with plastic wrap and refrigerate.

SOUR CREAM SAUCE
Cooking juices from the terrine
1 cup sour cream
2 egg yolks (optional)
1/2 cup heavy cream
1 teaspoon prepared horseradish
1/2 teaspoon prepared mustard
1/2 teaspoon lemon juice
Salt and pepper

Reduce cooking juices to 4 tablespoons. Pour into a mixing bowl, beat in 3 tablespoons sour cream and egg yolks. Stir in the rest of the sour cream and heavy cream and season with horseradish, mustard, lemon juice, salt, and pepper. Refrigerate until serving.

ROAST TURKEY WITH PORK SAUSAGE STUFFING AND CHESTNUTS
1 15-pound oven-ready turkey
Salt, pepper
Pork sausage stuffing (recipe follows)
6 tablespoons melted butter

Preheat oven to 325 degrees. Wash and dry the turkey and season the cavity with salt and pepper. Fill loosely with stuffing and truss. Rub the skin with melted butter and place, breast-side down, on a rack in a shallow roasting pan. Roast 2½ hours, basting often with butter. Turn breast side up and roast, basting frequently with butter and pan drippings, about 2 hours longer, or until the bird tests done. Let turkey stand in a warm place for 20 minutes before carving. Serve on a platter with mounded chestnuts. (Directions follow.)

PORK SAUSAGE AND CORNBREAD STUFFING

4 tablespoons unsalted butter
3 cups finely chopped yellow
  onions
1 pound lightly seasoned
  bulk sausage (breakfast
  sausage seasoned with sage
  is best)
3 cups coarsely crumbled cornbread
  (preferaby homemade)
3 cups coarsely crumbled
  wholewheat bread
3 cups coarsely crumbled
  French bread
2 teaspoons dried thyme
1 teaspoon dried sage
Salt and pepper
½ cup chopped parsley
1½ cups chopped, boiled chestnuts

Melt the butter in a skillet and add chopped onions. Cook over medium heat, partially covered, until tender and lightly browned. Put in a mixing bowl. Crumble the sausage into the skillet and cook over medium heat until lightly browned. Use a slotted spoon and add sausage to onions in the mixing bowl. Add the remaining ingredients to the mixing bowl and gently mix. Cool completely before stuffing the bird.

CHESTNUTS

1 pound fresh chestnuts

With a sharp knife, score the flat part of each chestnut with a cross. Place nuts in a large saucepan and cover with water. Boil nuts for 10 to 15 minutes. Peel them while they are still hot. Mound around the turkey to serve.

BOUDIN BLANC

Large sausage casings
¼ cup milk
¼ cup heavy cream
1 onion, finely chopped
¾ cup fresh bread crumbs
½ pound lean veal
½ pound fat pork
½ pound boned chicken, veal,
  or turkey
2 egg whites
1 teaspoon ground allspice
  Salt and white pepper
2 tablespoons butter
1½ quarts water
3 cups milk
1 carrot, diced
1 onion, diced
1 leek, trimmed, split and diced
1 stalk celery, diced
Salt and pepper

Serves 4 to 6

Soak sausage casings in cold water for several hours until pliable. Scald the milk and cream with the chopped onion and leave to infuse for 15 minutes. Strain the milk mixture over the bread crumbs and leave to cool. Work the veal, fat pork, and chicken twice through the fine plate of a grinder; then work it in 2 batches to a fine paste in a food processor. Put the mixture in a bowl and stir in the egg whites, soaked bread crumbs, allspice, and salt and white pepper. Sauté a small piece of the mixture and taste for seasoning. It should be quite spicy. Beat with a wooden spoon until very smooth. To fill the sausages, drain the casings. Insert a sausage stuffer or funnel at one end of one casing and spoon in the filling, pushing it down into the casing. (Casings tear easily and, filled too tightly, will burst during cooking.) Prick the sausages with a pin to remove air holes, and tie them at 6-inch intervals with string. To cook the sausages, bring the water and milk to a boil in a large pot with carrot, onion, leek, celery, salt, and pepper. Lower the sausages into the pot, cover and poach for 18 to 20 minutes at 195 degrees. Don't boil or sausages will burst. Let the sausages cool in the liquid and refrigerate overnight. To finish, drain the sausages, heat the butter in a skillet and fry them for 4 to 5 minutes or until very hot and golden. Alternatively, brush them with melted butter and broil. Serve hot.

CARAMELIZED APPLES

4 to 6 apples, Yellow Delicious
  or Winesap
3 tablespoons butter
¼ cup brown sugar
1½ tablespoons water
Cinnamon

Core apples and slice in rings or sections. Melt butter in an iron skillet, add apples, and sprinkle with brown sugar and cinna-

mon. Add water. Sauté for 15 to 20 minutes, turning gently several times.

CARROTS AU BEURRE

4 cups tender young carrots,
*   scraped and sliced*
¼ cup melted butter
1 cup light cream
½ teaspoon nutmeg
½ pound green beans, cut into
*   julienne slices and steamed*
*   until tender*
Slivered almonds

Serves 8

Cook carrots in salted water until a fork will break them. Purée them using a food mill. Add butter, cream, and nutmeg. Mound lightly in the center of a vegetable platter and surround with julienne green beans. Garnish with slivered almonds.

PEARS IN ORANGE JUICE

8 firm but ripe Bartlett pears
*   of uniform size*
1 cup sugar
3 cups water
1 tablespoon lemon juice
1 cup fresh orange juice
1 tablespoon curaçao or Cointreau
Peel of one orange

Peel pears and remove bud ends but leave stems on. Make a thin syrup with sugar, water, and lemon juice. Cover the pears and stew gently in syrup until tender but still firm, about 20 minutes. Remove pears and arrange on a serving dish, stem ends up. Boil down the syrup, then add orange juice and curaçao or Cointreau. Pour

syrup mixture over pears. Remove the peel of one orange making sure not to lift any of the white membrane. Cut the rind into tiny slivers and scatter over pears.

FRIANDISES AUX AMANDES

½ cup grated, blanched almonds
½ cup granulated sugar
4 egg whites
3 tablespoons flour
½ teaspoon vanilla extract
½ cup butter

Makes 24

Cook butter slowly until slightly browned. Let cool. Mix together almonds and sugar. Add egg whites a little at a time, beating well after each addition. Stir in flour, vanilla, and gently fold in the browned butter. Turn batter into small buttered and floured molds and bake at 350 degrees for 8 to 10 minutes. Remove the friands from the molds to a rack to cool. Serve with black rind cheese.

CHOCOLATE HAZELNUT CAKE

GÉNOISE

3 ounces semisweet chocolate
*   pieces*
½ teaspoon cinnamon
3 tablespoons water
2 ounces hazelnuts
6 tablespoons granulated sugar
3 eggs, separated
¼ cup potato starch
Pinch of salt

CHOCOLATE BUTTER CREAM:

6 ounces semisweet chocolate
*   pieces*
4 tablespoons water
½ teaspoon cinnamon
2 eggs, separated
8 tablespoons cold butter
Pinch of salt
¼ cup granulated sugar
¼ cup kirsch or cognac
12-14 toasted hazelnuts, split
*   in half*

Serves 8

Butter sides of an 8-inch cake pan and line the bottom with a piece of buttered wax paper. Preheat the oven to 350 degrees.

For the genoise, place the chocolate, cinnamon, and water in a heavy-bottomed saucepan over low heat and allow the chocolate to melt, stirring occasionally until it is smooth. While the chocolate melts, pulverize the hazelnuts in a blender. In a mixing bowl, gradually beat 3 tablespoons of the sugar into the egg yolks, working them until they have thickened and are pale in color. Stir the hazelnuts and potato starch into the egg mixture, and then the warm chocolate. Beat the egg whites with a pinch of salt until they form soft peaks; sprinkle on the remaining 3 tablespoons sugar and continue beating until stiff peaks are formed. Delicately fold the chocolate and hazelnut mixture into the beaten whites and turn the batter into the prepared pan.

Bake the cake 18 to 20 minutes, until it is just set and it is beginning to pull away from the sides of the pan. Allow the cake to cool on a rack for at least 10 minutes before unmolding it to finish cooling on the rack.

For the chocolate butter cream, melt the chocolate with water and cinnamon. When it is smooth, remove the pan from the heat and stir in the egg yolks, one at a time. Return the pan to low heat and stir continuously for 1 to 2 minutes. Remove from heat; stir in the butter, a tablespoon at a time. Beat the egg whites with the pinch of salt and then the sugar, to form a light meringue, as directed above. Fold the warm chocolate mixture into the meringue and set the cream in the refrigerator or freezer until it is set. When the cake is completely cool, slice it in half horizontally, using a serrated knife, and sprinkle the cut surfaces with brandy. Assemble the cake, filling the center with a generous layer of butter cream, and allowing it to firm up in the refrigerator before spreading the top and sides of the cake with the remaining cream. Garnish with hazelnuts. Chill until ready to serve.

SAVARIN

1 cup milk
1 envelope dry yeast
¼ cup warm water
½ cup sugar
½ teaspoon salt
⅔ cup butter, melted and
   slightly cooled
4 eggs
3½ cups flour, or as needed
Whipped cream

SYRUP:

1 cup sugar
2 cups water
1 cup kirsch, rum, or cognac
Juice of ½ lemon

Scald the milk and pour it into a large, warm bowl. Dissolve yeast in warm water with 1 tablespoon of sugar. When the milk is lukewarm, add yeast and salt. Beat the eggs and remaining sugar together and add butter. Add egg mixture to yeast mixture. Add enough flour to make a heavy, thick batter. Beat for 5 minutes with a wooden spoon.

Cover with a cloth and set in a warm place to rise until doubled in bulk, about 1½ hours. Punch dough down. Butter an 11-inch ring mold and fill the ring a little less than half full. Cover and let dough rise until doubled in bulk. Bake in a preheated 350-degree oven for 35 minutes. Cool in ring.

Prepare the syrup: Simmer water and sugar for 10 minutes, and cool. Add liquor and lemon juice. Remove cake from mold, pour ¼ cup of the syrup over the top, and put cake back into mold. With a skewer make deep holes in the cake and pour in remaining syrup until well soaked. Let soak for several hours. Serve with a bowl of sweetened whipped cream flavored with the same liquor as the syrup. Fill center with fresh or brandied fruit.

Supper By the Hearth

Whether you have a fireplace or not, this is a cozy meal that's good on any winter night. With no fussy food that can't be kept waiting, it's ideal for a family supper or an informal get-together on a busy preholiday evening.

NEW ENGLAND FISH CHOWDER

This flavorful chowder is best made a full day ahead and reheated just before serving.

¼ pound salt pork, diced
2 onions, chopped
4 cups water
3 cups thinly sliced potatoes
3 pounds cod, flounder, or
*   haddock, cut into chunks*
3 cups milk
1 cup light cream
Salt and pepper to taste

Serves 8 to 10

In a large soup kettle, render the pork. Remove some of the fat if necessary, leaving just enough to fry the onions. Add the onion to the kettle and fry until soft. Add the potatoes and water, cover the kettle, and boil gently for 15 minutes. Place the fish in the kettle on top of the potatoes, cover, reduce the heat and simmer for 15 minutes. Add the milk and cream. Season to taste with salt and pepper. Remove the kettle from the heat and set aside, covered, to allow the flavors to blend.

Reheat just before serving.

CORN STICKS

Special cast-iron pans with molds are needed to make these corn sticks; they should be well-seasoned, greased with lard or oil, and heated until almost smoking before the corn-stick batter is poured into them for baking. Lacking the molds, a large iron skillet can be used for a different, but nevertheless delicious, bread. Corn sticks are best served right out of the oven.

1½ cups white cornmeal
1½ cups boiling water
3 eggs, well beaten
1 tablespoon butter, melted
1½ cups milk
2 teaspoons salt

Serves 8 to 10

Preheat the oven to 400 degrees. Grease and preheat 3 corn-stick molds.

Place the cornmeal in a bowl and gradually pour in the boiling water, stirring until the mixture is smooth. Cool to lukewarm. Add the eggs, beating until smooth, then the butter, milk, and salt.

Fill the prepared corn-stick irons three-quarters full, and bake until the corn sticks are lightly browned (about 30 minutes). Turn the corn sticks out of the molds immediately.

GLAZED PORK LOIN

3 pounds pork loin, boned and tied
½ cup Dijon mustard
½ cup dark brown sugar
2 tablespoons vegetable oil
½ cup bourbon whiskey
Salt and pepper to taste
2 cups tiny white onions
1 cup pitted prunes
1½ cups rich beef stock
½ teaspoon cornstarch (optional)

Serves 8 to 10

Dry the pork loin thoroughly with paper towels. Paint one side with mustard and coat with brown sugar; turn the loin over and repeat.

In a heavy skillet or roasting pan, heat the oil. Brown the meat in it, turning it when one side is colored so that it browns evenly. Keep turning the meat until it is well browned on all sides; the sugar will caramelize; watch carefully to see that it does not burn. Pour half the whiskey over the meat and ignite it. When the flame goes out, season the pork to taste with salt and pepper. Add ½ cup of the beef stock to the pan, cover, and simmer over low heat (or place the covered pan in a preheated 350-degree oven). Check the meat from time to time to make sure there is sufficient liquid in the pan. After 45 minutes turn the meat over. The pork is done when juices run clear when it is pierced with a knife.

While the meat is cooking, peel the onions. Put them in a saucepan with ½ cup of the beef stock and simmer over moderate heat until the onions are barely tender. Remove from the heat and let the onions cool in the stock.

In a small bowl, place the prunes to steep in the remaining ½ cup of stock.

When the meat is done, remove it to a warm platter and cover loosely with foil. Skim as much fat as possible from the cooking liquid, set the pan over the heat, add the remaining whiskey and the drained liquid from the prunes and onions. Bring to a boil, stirring to dislodge the sediment in the pan. Boil and stir until the sauce is smooth. (It can be thickened, if desired, by adding the cornstarch dissolved in a little water.)

Add the prunes and onions to the pan and simmer for a few minutes until they are heated through. When ready to serve, slice part of the pork, garnish the platter with the prunes and onions, and serve with the sauce from the pan.

BAKED BEANS, BOSTON STYLE

This recipe fills a 2-quart bean pot, enough baked beans to serve a dozen hungry people and still have leftovers, which can be reheated another day. (The New England friend who shared the recipe with us likes baked beans cold, for breakfast. And a young man we know likes them cold on buttered toast for lunch or a snack.) For a smaller group, divide the ingredients in half and bake in a 1-quart pot or covered casserole.

2 pounds dried white beans
(California pea beans or
New York State white
beans, if available)
1 teaspoon baking soda
1 pound salt pork
1 medium onion
½ cup sugar
⅔ cup molasses
2 teaspoons dry mustard
4 teaspoons salt
½ teaspoon pepper

Serves 12 to 15

Soak the beans overnight. In the morning, parboil them for 10 minutes with the baking soda.

Preheat the oven to 300 degrees. Drain the beans in a colander and rinse with cold water. Cut the salt pork in half and score the rind in deep 1-inch squares. Place half on the bottom of a 2-quart bean pot with the whole onion. Add the beans and place the remaining pork on top. In a small bowl, combine the sugar, molasses, mustard, salt, and pepper and spoon over the beans. Bake covered for 6 hours, adding water as needed. The liquid should barely cover the beans until about half an hour before serving. At that point, let the liquid cook down to form a brown crust on the top of the beans.

COLE SLAW

1 small head green cabbage
1/2 cup chopped scallion
    (or onion)
1 tablespoon celery seed
Salt
Freshly ground black pepper

Serves 12

Cut the cabbage into quarters, remove the white core, and shred the remainder very fine. Add the chopped scallion and celery seed. Season with salt and pepper to taste, and toss with one of the following dressings:

BACON DRESSING

2 strips bacon
1 teaspoon cornstarch
1/2 cup water
1/2 cup cider vinegar
1 tablespoon sugar (or to taste)
Salt, if needed

Chop the bacon, place in a heavy pan, and fry until crisp. Remove and drain. Pour all but 1 table-spoon of the fat from the pan, stir in the cornstarch until blended, and add the water. Bring to a boil over moderate heat, stirring constantly. As the mixture begins to thicken, gradually add the vine-gar, and stir until smooth and thick. Season to taste with sugar—the amount needed will depend on the strength of the vinegar—and add salt if needed. Pour over the shredded cabbage, toss, and serve.

SOUR CREAM DRESSING

Combine equal parts of home-made mayonnaise and sour cream. Season to taste with salt, pepper, and Dijon mustard. Add just enough to the shredded cabbage to moisten and season.

BLACK WALNUT CAKE

The unusual, slightly acrid taste of black walnuts permeates this cake. Many people love it, but if you're not one of them, substitute regular English walnuts. Make the whipped cream to finish the cake just before serving

3/4 cup butter, softened
1 cup sugar
2 eggs
1 cup sour cream
1 teaspoon baking soda
1 3/4 cups flour
2 teaspoons baking powder
1 cup finely chopped black walnuts
1 cup whipping cream
1/2 teaspoon vanilla extract
1 tablespoon extra fine sugar
    (or to taste)
1/4 cup coarsely chopped
    black walnuts

Preheat the oven to 325 degrees. Butter and flour a 9-inch square pan and set aside.

In a large bowl, cream together the butter and sugar until the mixture is very light. Add the eggs, one at a time, beating after each addition. In a small bowl, combine the sour cream and baking soda. Mix well then add to the butter mixture. Sift together the flour and baking powder and add to the batter. Stir in the 1 cup of finely chopped black walnuts. Pour the batter into the prepared pan and bake for 40 to 50 minutes, or until the cake tests done. Place the cake pan on a rack and let stand for 10 minutes. Run a knife around the edges of the pan to loosen the cake, then carefully turn it out onto the rack to cool.

When the cake is thoroughly cooled, cut it in half vertically, then cut each half horizontally to make four 4½x9-inch layers. Whip the cream, stir in the vanilla, then sweeten to taste with sugar.

Place one of the cake layers on a serving dish, spread with whipped cream, and cover with another layer of cake, pressing it firmly into place. Spread with cream, and continue until all the layers are used. Frost the top and sides of the cake with the remaining whipped cream, garnish with the coarsely chopped nuts, and store in a cool place until serving time.

APPLE TARTS
1⅓ cups unbleached flour
1 teaspoon salt
½ cup unsalted butter, chilled
¼ cup (or slightly more) ice water
3 to 4 firm cooking apples (Granny Smith is a good choice)
Juice of ½ lemon
Sugar
Apricot jam

Makes two 8-inch tarts
Place flour and salt in a bowl and, using a pastry blender, cut in the chilled butter until the mixture resembles coarse meal. Sprinkle on the iced water and stir quickly with a fork until the mixture holds together, adding additional drops of water if needed. Gather the pastry into a ball, flatten, wrap securely in plastic, and chill for at least half an hour.

When you are ready to bake the tarts, preheat the oven to 400 degrees. Peel the apples, cut them in halves, and remove the cores. Slice the halves into a bowl, keeping the pieces thin and as uniform as possible; as they accumulate, sprinkle with lemon juice to keep them from darkening. Add sugar to taste and set aside.

Divide the pastry in half and roll out to fit two 8-inch tart pans with removable bottoms. Brush the pastry with apricot jam, and arrange the apple slices, slightly overlapping, in circles around the pastry. Bake until the pastry is brown. Remove the tarts to a rack to cool, and brush the top while still hot with a little additional jam to give the tarts a good glaze. Serve warm or cold.

JOE FROGGERS
These spicy molasses cookies are a specialty of Marblehead, Massachusetts, where nearly everyone seems to have an "authentic" recipe for the original version, said to have been made by a man named Joe, who lived near a frog pond. The cookies are round and fat, a little like the frogs in Joe's pond, hence the name. Some versions are flavored with rum, some not. This may or may not be the original recipe, but it makes very good cookies, which, if stored in a tightly covered tin, will keep fresh for several weeks.

2¾ cups flour
3 teaspoons baking powder
¼ teaspoon baking soda
¼ teaspoon ground cloves
1 teaspoon ground ginger
1 scant tablespoon cinnamon
½ cup butter, softened
1 cup dark brown sugar
⅔ cup molasses

Makes 2½ dozen
Preheat the oven to 375 degrees.

Sift together the flour, baking powder, baking soda, cloves, ginger, and cinnamon. In a large bowl, cream the butter and brown sugar together until smooth, then stir in the molasses. Add the flour and spice mixture to the bowl and, using both hands, mix until all the flour has been worked in and the dough is smooth. Divide the dough in half, and roll out a half at a time to ⅓-inch thick. If the dough seems sticky or is difficult to handle, let it firm up in the refrigerator for 15 or 20 minutes.

Cut the dough out in circles, as large as you like, arrange them on baking sheets, and bake until lightly browned. Cool the cookies on a rack, and store tightly covered.

Hogmanay: A Scottish New Year's Eve Party

"A gude New Year to one an a' and mony may ye see!" is one of the greetings that ushers in several nights of jubilant celebrating in every Scottish village and town as the New Year begins. Hogmanay, the Scottish term that actually means "Old Year's Night," became one of the most festive holidays in Scotland when the Reformation forbade celebrations of Christmas. Scots, not to be deprived of their winter holiday, circumvented the ban by making merry at the New Year instead.

Long before the hour of midnight, however, preparations begin—the traditional array of Hogmanay dishes is baked, boiled, or brewed. All is made ready so that at the last stroke of twelve the celebration begins in earnest. Everyone participates; some going forth to visit friends, walking or riding through the streets, many carrying copper kettles of het pint, offering a cup against the cold to all passersby. Others stay at home, anxiously waiting to welcome the "first footer," the first person to cross the threshold in the New Year, because it is he or she who will determine the family fortune for the coming twelve months. A tall, dark stranger, preferably male, assures good luck; a man or a woman with blond or red hair bodes ill. The first footer brings good Scotch whiskey to share with his hosts as well as a gift of food, usually cake or bread, and a lump of coal, which he tosses into the fire, calling out, "Lang may your lum reek!" (Long may your hearth burn!) Festivities continue with music and dancing, along with drinking and eating a wonderful choice of Scottish dishes: black bun, bridies, petticoat tails, oat cakes, godcakes, and lots of shortbread. Atholl brose, good Scotch whiskey, and more het pint are offered, too.

MENU

Hogmanay Shortbread
Petticoat Tails
Trifle
Godcakes
Black Bun
Lemon Curd
Atholl Brose
Het Pint

Hogmanay Shortbread

Scottish shortbread is thick and is not rolled out into biscuits. This recipe makes a reasonable amount of delicious shortbread, but you may want to double the proportions so you'll have enough to serve hungry holiday visitors.

1 cup unsalted butter
1/2 cup powdered sugar
2 cups flour, unsifted
1/4 cup cornstarch
Light cream
Granulated sugar, for sprinkling

Serves 10 to 12

Preheat the oven to 300 degrees.

In a large bowl, blend the butter and sugar. Add the flour and the cornstarch. Mix thoroughly. The results are best when an electric mixer is used. Add the cream a tablespoon at a time until the dough gathers into one clump, but keep it as dry as you can.

Press the dough into a 10-inch-square, ungreased pan. With a fork, prick the dough all over. Bake for about 40 minutes, or until the shortbread is very pale tan.

Remove the shortbread from the oven and without taking it out of the pan, cut it into serving-size squares or rectangles. Sprinkle the shortbread with granulated sugar and put the pan back into the oven. Reduce the heat to 275 degrees, and bake the shortbread for another 30 to 40 minutes, or until it is golden. Turn the oven off, but do not remove the pan until the shortbread is cold.

Petticoat Tails

These cakes taste best if they are baked a week before serving and stored in an airtight tin. The name may come from the French *petites gâtelles*, meaning "little cakes," or from the way they are cut to resemble a ruffled hoop petticoat.

2 cups flour
Pinch of salt
3 tablespoons granulated sugar
2 tablespoons milk
1/2 cup unsalted butter
1 teaspoon caraway seeds
(optional)
Granulated sugar, for sprinkling

Preheat the oven to 325 degrees. Using butter, lightly grease a baking sheet.

Into a large bowl sift the flour, salt, and sugar. In a small saucepan, combine the milk and butter. Cook over low heat, stirring, until the butter just melts. Mix into the dry ingredients. Work with your hands to form a smooth dough. Work in the caraway seeds, if desired.

Turn the dough onto a floured board. Roll it into a circle 8 to 10 inches in diameter. Place on the prepared baking sheet. From the center of the dough, cut out a circle about 3 inches in diameter. Then make cuts in the dough, from the outer edge to the center ring, to make 8 even pieces.

Bake for 30 to 40 minutes, or until the petticoat tails are golden. Remove the baking sheet from the oven. Sprinkle sugar over the cakes, then transfer them to a wire rack to cool.

Trifle

This is a popular Scottish dessert. It has many variations, and there is no way to fail with it.

Pound cake or ladyfingers
1/2 cup raspberry jam
1/2 cup sweet sherry or fruit juice
4 egg yolks
2 tablespoons sugar
2 1/2 cups milk
1/2 teaspoon vanilla extract
1/2 pint whipping cream

Garnishes:
Macaroon crumbs, fresh fruit in season, toasted almonds, glacé cherries, angelica

Spread slices of pound cake or ladyfingers with jam, and with the jam side inward line the bottom and sides of a glass serving dish with them. Sprinkle the cake with the sherry or fruit juice.

In the top of a double boiler, beat the egg yolks and sugar together. In a small saucepan, warm the milk, but do not allow it to boil. Stir the warm milk into the egg mixture. When it is well blended, set the top of the double boiler into the bottom, in which water is simmering. Cook, stirring constantly, until the custard is thick. Remove from the heat, mix in the vanilla extract; set aside to cool.

When the custard is almost set, pour it over the pieces of cake in the serving dish. Whip the cream and spread it on top of the custard layer. Decorate with any of the garnishes, or to suit your own fancy.

GODCAKES

Traditional since the Middle Ages, these pastries are said to have been given to children by their godparents as a New Year's gift for good luck. This is a shortcut version, particularly welcome during the busy holiday season.

1½ pounds prepared puff pastry
(available in the freezer case
of the supermarket)
1 pound mincemeat
1 egg white
Granulated sugar

Preheat the oven to 425 degrees.

On a floured board, roll out the puff pastry to a thickness of about ⅛ inch. Cut the pastry into rectangles that are about 6 by 8 inches. Put a generous spoonful of the mincemeat in the center of each rectangle. Fold each rectangle of pastry over to make an elongated triangle. Seal the edges with the tines of a fork. Make three small slits (said to represent the Holy Trinity) in the top of each, then place them on a baking sheet.

Bake for about 15 minutes, or until the cakes are well risen and golden. Meanwhile, in a small bowl, beat the egg white until it is frothy.

When the cakes are baked, brush each one with egg white and sprinkle with sugar. Return them to the oven for about 3 minutes.

Cool the cakes on a wire rack and eat them as soon as possible.

SCOTS BLACK BUN

"Bun" is an old Scottish word for plum cake, or fruitcake. It is traditionally encased in a pastry shell and can be made a week or two ahead of time and stored in an airtight tin in a cool place. At New Year's parties in Scotland, great slices of Black Bun are washed down with swallows of "het pint" to fortify the Hogmanay visitors against the highland chill.

PASTRY
3 cups flour
6 tablespoons lard or vegetable
shortening
6 tablespoons margarine
Ice water

CAKE
1⅔ cups raisins
1⅔ cups dried currants
4 ounces mixed diced fruits
4 ounces shredded almonds
2½ cups flour
½ teaspoon baking soda
1 teaspoon ground cinnamon
½ teaspoon ground nutmeg
1 teaspoon ground ginger
Pinch of cayenne pepper
¾ cup brown sugar
2 eggs
4 tablespoons light cream
2 tablespoons brandy
1 egg, well beaten

First make the pastry. Pour the flour into a large bowl. Using two table knives or a pastry blender, cut the lard, or vegetable shortening, and the margarine into the flour. When the mixture resembles meal, moisten it with only enough ice water to make a stiff dough. Gather the dough into a clump. Roll out two-thirds of it into a large circle. Line a 9-inch springform pan with it. Roll out the remaining dough into a circle that is about 9½ inches in diameter. Set aside.

Preheat the oven to 325 degrees.

To make the cake, in a large bowl combine the raisins, currants, mixed fruits, and almonds. Into another large bowl, sift the flour, baking soda, cinnamon, nutmeg, ginger, and cayenne pepper together. Stir in the brown sugar, dried fruits, and almonds. Add the 2 eggs, cream, and brandy and stir to a firm batter.

Carefully put the batter into the pastry-lined pan. Cover with the remaining circle of pastry, sealing and trimming the edges. Using a metal skewer, make 5 or 6 holes through the pastry lid right down to the bottom of the cake. Brush the pastry lid with the beaten egg. Bake in the middle of the oven for 2 to 2½ hours. Test with a straw, and when the cake is done remove the pan from the oven. Cool the cake in the pan on a rack. Store the Black Bun in the pan, covered tightly with foil, in a cool place until Hogmanay.

LEMON CURD

This is a smooth and delicious spread for plain crackers or buttered toast. It can also be used to fill small tart shells or as the filling for a lemon meringue pie. When you've run out of other treats, it's a grand thing to find a jar of lemon curd in the refrigerator where it will keep for up to a month if it is tightly covered.

1 cup butter
1½ cups granulated sugar
Juice and finely grated rind
    of 4 large lemons
4 large eggs, beaten

Makes 3 cups

Cut the butter into small pieces and put them into the top part of a double boiler over simmering water. Add the sugar, lemon juice, and lemon rind and stir constantly until all the ingredients are well blended. Still stirring, pour a little of the lemon mixture into the beaten eggs. Then pour all the egg and lemon mixture into the top of the double boiler. Stir until the mixture thickens. It may take up to 10 minutes.

Pour the lemon curd into warm, clean jars; cover and store in the refrigerator.

ATHOLL BROSE

This potent beverage is believed to have originated when the Earl of Atholl captured the Earl of Ross by filling the well at which he was wont to drink with this concoction. It is another drink that sustains the Scots during their Hogmanay rounds.

3 ounces steel-cut oatmeal
2 tablespoons honey
Scotch whiskey

Mix the oatmeal with enough water to make a thin gruel. Set aside for 30 minutes.

Strain off the water into a quart jar, pressing the oatmeal well to get out all of the liquid. Add the honey. Stir with a silver spoon until the mixture is smooth. Fill the jar with whiskey and seal it.

Shake well before each serving.

HET PINT

Made good and hot just before the hour of midnight, Het Pint was served to the first footers when they made their Hogmanay visits. The proportions vary according to the region of Scotland where it is made, but as long as you follow the general directions, you can make the drink to suit your own palate. It is tasty and potent.

1 egg
10 ounces mild Scottish ale
½ whole nutmeg, grated
Sugar to taste
2 to 3 ounces Scotch whiskey
    or brandy

In a large bowl, beat the egg. Set aside. Pour the ale into a saucepan. Grate in the nutmeg and add sugar to taste. Heat until very hot but not boiling. Take the pan off the heat and pour some of the hot ale over the beaten egg, stirring all the while. Strain the mixture back into the pan and add the whiskey. Heat again, but do not boil. Pour into a pitcher, and then pour back and forth several times until there is a good froth. Drink hot.

Holiday Desserts

The Christmas season is a time when most people forget about their waistlines and indulge themselves in the rich and luscious desserts from which they abstain the rest of the year. These desserts are very special. Most of them entail a bit of work, but the results and the compliments from friends and family make it worth the effort.

BLACK FOREST CHERRY CAKE

This is an elaborate cake, a creation that in itself can become a part of holiday tradition.

11 tablespoons unsalted butter, softened
6 tablespoons flour
6 eggs, at room temperature
1 teaspoon vanilla extract
1 cup sugar
½ cup sifted flour
½ cup unsweetened cocoa

Serves 12

With a paper towel, lightly grease the bottoms and sides of three 8-inch round cake pans with 1 tablespoon of butter. Sprinkle 2 tablespoons of flour into each pan. Tip each pan from side to side to spread the flour evenly, then invert it and rap it sharply on a table to remove any excess flour. Set the pans aside. Preheat the oven to 350 degrees.

In a small saucepan, melt the remaining 10 tablespoons of butter over very low heat. Remove the pan from the heat, let the butter rest for 1 minute, then skim off the foam. Pour the clear butter into a small bowl and set aside. Discard the milky solids at the bottom of the pan.

In the bowl of an electric mixer, combine the eggs, vanilla, and sugar. Beat at high speed until the mixture is thick and fluffy, about 10 minutes. Combine the flour and cocoa in a sifter and sift, a little at a time, over the egg mixture, folding it in gently with a rubber spatula. Finally, add the clarified butter 2 tablespoons at a time. Do not overmix.

Gently pour the batter into the prepared pans and bake in the middle of the oven for 10 to 15 minutes, or until a cake tester comes out clean. Remove the cakes from the oven and let them cook in the pans for 5 minutes, then turn them out onto racks.

SYRUP

¾ cup sugar
1 cup cold water
⅓ cup kirsch

In a small saucepan, combine the sugar and water. Bring to a boil over moderate heat, stirring only until the sugar dissolves. Then boil briskly, uncovered, for 5 minutes. Remove the pan from the heat. When the syrup has cooled to lukewarm, mix in the kirsch.

Put a long strip of wax paper on a work surface. Transfer the cakes to the wax paper. With the tines of a long fork, prick each cake lightly in several places.

Sprinkle the layers evenly with the syrup. Let them rest for at least 5 minutes.

FILLING AND TOPPING

3 cups chilled heavy cream
1/2 cup powdered sugar
1/4 cup kirsch
1 cup canned dark cherries, drained
Maraschino cherries with stems, drained and rinsed
6 ounces semisweet bar chocolate

In a large chilled bowl, beat the cream with a rotary beater until it thickens slightly. Sift the powdered sugar over the cream and continue beating until the cream forms firm peaks when the beater is lifted. Pour in the kirsch in a thin stream. Beat only until the kirsch is absorbed.

To assemble the cake, place one layer in the center of a serving plate. With a spatula, spread the top with 1/2 inch of whipped cream and strew with 1/2 cup of the drained canned cherries leaving a 1/2-inch border of cream. Gently set a second layer on top of the cherries and repeat the procedure. Set the third layer in place and spread the top and sides of the cake with the remaining cream.

Holding the chocolate over wax paper and using a sharp, narrow-bladed vegetable peeler, shave it into thin curls. Gently press the curls into the side of the cake. Arrange a few curls and maraschino cherries on top.

BÛCHE DE NOËL

Another dessert to applaud, the Yule Log appears (and disappears) only at Christmas.

1 1/2 tablespoons unsweetened cocoa
9 tablespoons flour
Pinch salt
6 eggs, separated
1/3 teaspoon cream of tartar
1 1/3 cup granulated sugar
3/4 teaspoon vanilla extract

Grease a jelly-roll pan with butter, then flour it lightly and set aside. Preheat the oven to 325 degrees.

Sift the cocoa with the flour and the salt twice. Set aside.

In a large bowl, with a rotary beater, beat the egg whites with the cream of tartar until they hold stiff peaks. Gradually beat in half the sugar. Continue beating until the mixture is very glossy and again holds stiff peaks.

In another large bowl, beat the egg yolks until thick. Gradually beat in the remaining sugar and the vanilla. Continue beating until the mixture is thick and light colored.

Using a metal spoon, into the egg mixture carefully fold in the flour mixture alternating with the egg whites until blended. Pour the batter into the prepared jelly roll pan and bake for 25 minutes. Turn the cake out immediately on a board covered with wax paper. Trim all the edges of the cake. Cover the top with wax paper, then carefully roll the cake into a log shape. Set aside to cool.

FILLING

3 squares (3 ounces) semisweet chocolate
2 egg yolks
1/4 cup granulated sugar
1/4 cup water
1 cup unsalted butter, softened
2 teaspoons instant coffee

In the top of a double boiler, over simmering water, melt the chocolate. Set aside.

In a small bowl, beat the egg yolks lightly until mixed.

In a small saucepan, combine the sugar and the water. Bring to a boil until it reaches the thread stage (230 degrees on a candy thermometer).

Gradually pour the hot syrup on the egg yolks, beating hard. Continue to beat until the mixture is cool, thick, and light.

In a large bowl, cream the butter. Add the egg yolk mixture, the coffee, and the chocolate, beating until light and creamy.

Unroll the cake. Remove the top layer of wax paper. Spread the cake with the filling. Carefully roll the cake again into a log shape, removing the bottom layer of wax paper as you roll.

CHOCOLATE CREAM

12 squares (12 ounces) semisweet chocolate
1/4 cup unsalted butter, softened
1 1/4 cups heavy cream
1/4 cup amaretto
Glacé cherries
Candied angelica

In the top of a double boiler over simmering water, melt the chocolate. Remove from the heat and beat in the butter one tablespoon at a time. Set aside to cool.

In a large bowl, combine the cream and the amaretto. Whip until the mixture holds soft peaks. Add the chocolate and continue beating until the mixture holds stiff peaks. Spoon the chocolate cream into a pastry bag fitted with a large star tip.

Cut a slice from each end of the log. Place the log on a serving plate, then arrange each end slice on opposite sides to look like a cut log. Pipe the cream over the length of the cake to simulate bark. Spread the cream on the log ends in a circular motion. Decorate with the cherries and the candied angelica cut to look like holly leaves.

BULLY PUDDING

1/2 cup sugar
1/4 cup butter
1/2 teaspoon baking powder
2 eggs
1 cup milk
1 teaspoon vanilla extract
2 cups chopped, pitted dates
1/4 cup flour
2 cups coarsely chopped walnuts

Grease a shallow casserole with butter. Preheat the oven to 300 degrees.

In a large bowl, cream the butter and the sugar. Add the baking powder, eggs, and milk and mix well. Add the vanilla. Dust the dates with flour so the pieces don't stick together. Add the dates and the nuts to the mixture. Pour into the casserole and bake for 40 minutes, or until the custard sets.

CHOCOLATE ROLL

1/2 pound best available
*   semisweet chocolate*
9 extra large eggs, separated
1/2 teaspoon cream of tartar
1/2 cup superfine sugar
1 teaspoon vanilla extract
2 tablespoons Kahlua

Preheat the oven to 350 degrees. Butter a 13x18-inch baking pan. Line the pan with a sheet of buttered wax paper. Put a sheet of foil the size of the pan on a work surface. Dust it with powdered sugar.

Melt the chocolate in the top of a double boiler over gently simmering water. Set aside to cool.

In a large bowl, beat the egg whites with the cream of tartar until stiff peaks form.

In another large bowl, beat the egg yolks with the sugar until the mixture is pale yellow and forms a ribbon when dropped from a spoon. Mix in the vanilla and the Kahlua. Fold in the melted chocolate. Then fold in the egg whites. Spread the batter in the prepared pan and bake for 15 minutes.

Turn the cake out on the foil and allow it to cool to room temperature before filling.

FILLING
2 1/2 cups heavy cream
1 teaspoon vanilla extract
1/3 cup powdered sugar

Whip the cream. When soft peaks form when the beater is lifted, gradually beat in the vanilla and powdered sugar. Spread the cream mixture over the cooled cake. Using the prepared foil, roll the cake from the long side until it forms a roll. Dust top with powdered sugar. Fold the foil over the cake, then seal the edges. Refrigerate until just before serving.

Festive Bowls

The phrase "a bowl of punch" was commonly used in seventeenth-century England and has been translated into other languages, including Dutch, German, and French. Punch came to America with the colonists, and by the eighteenth century was an established drink at most social occasions.

FISH HOUSE PUNCH

This is the treasured recipe of the oldest continually meeting social club in the English-speaking world, the State in Schuylkill, founded by a group of fun-loving Philadelphians in 1732. Membership in the club was and remains small—thirty members and ten apprentices—but over the years some illustrious guests have sampled the famous punch, among them George Washington.

¾ pound sugar
1 quart lemon juice
2 quarts Jamaica rum
1 quart cognac
2 quarts water
½ cup peach brandy

Serves 30

Dissolve the sugar in the water. Add the remaining ingredients and pour over a large block of ice in a punch bowl. Allow the punch to mellow for 2 hours, stirring it occasionally to ensure a perfect blend.

CHATHAM ARTILLERY PUNCH

Some recipes for punch are associated with groups, like this one adopted by Veterans of the Revolution in Chatham County, Georgia. Indeed, this recipe is of regimental proportions—it serves more than 100 people. Quarter it for about 40 guests.

1 pound green tea
2 gallons cold water
Juice of 36 lemons
5 pounds brown sugar
2 quarts maraschino cherries,
*   without stems and drained*
3 gallons Catawba wine
1 gallon rum
1 gallon brandy
1 gallon rye whiskey
1 gallon gin
12 quarts champagne

Steep the tea in the cold water overnight, then strain it. Mix the tea and lemon juice together, add the sugar, cherries, Catawba wine, rum, brandy, whiskey, and gin.

Cover the bowl and allow the mixture to ripen for at least 1 week.

When ready to serve, pour the punch over a block of ice in a punch bowl. Add the champagne at the last, stirring well.

RED PUNCH FOR CHRISTMAS

This punch is elegant and delicious. It is pictured above left in an antique English silver punch bowl, the base of which is decorated with camellias and sprigs of heather. For a smaller quantity, use 1 quart apple juice, 1 cup applejack, ½ cup sloe gin, and 1 bottle champagne.

1 quart applejack
2 cups sloe gin
2 quarts apple juice
2 bottles champagne
Juice of 1 lemon
Strawberries, sliced kiwi, fresh
*   mint leaves*

Serves 30

Chill all the ingredients. Combine them in a punch bowl just before serving. Add ice cubes. Float the fruit and mint leaves on top.

WASSAIL

In Old English and several Teutonic languages, "wassail" was a greeting, "to be in good health." By the twelfth century, however, wassailing was synonymous with drinking and carousing and was thought, at least by Norman conquerors, to be characteristic of the English. Early recipes for wassail included pieces of toasted bread, giving rise to the notion that when you make a "toast" with your cup, you are, without knowing it, referring back to that ancient drink.

6 small apples, cored but unpeeled
3 pints unchilled ale
¾ cup brown sugar
1 teaspoon each ground ginger,
*   cinnamon, nutmeg*
6 cloves
6 thin strips lemon peel
1 pint dry sherry

Serves 8

Place the apples in a baking pan. Bake them in a 300-degree oven, without water or sugar, until they are soft but the skin is not split.

In a large pan, combine 1 pint of ale with the brown sugar, spices, and lemon peel. Simmer

for 20 minutes. Add the sherry and the remaining pints of ale. Heat, but do not boil.

Serve the wassail in a large punch bowl or in individual glass beer mugs or heavy goblets, with an apple in each. Put a heavy silver serving spoon in each mug or goblet as you pour in the wassail.

HIPPOCRAS

Spiced wine predates history. One version probably got its name from the fabric bag, known as Hippocrates's sleeve, through which it was strained. This Hippocras was adapted from a "receipt" written down in the seventeenth century by William Penn's first wife, Gulielma. It may be served hot or chilled, depending on the weather and your preference.

2 quarts red wine (claret is best)
1 teaspoon ground ginger
½ teaspoon ground nutmeg
2 tablespoons ground cinnamon
6 whole peppercorns, ground
¼ teaspoon ground cloves
⅛ teaspoon crushed dried rosemary
1 cup sugar, or to taste

Serves 8

Pour the wine into a large glass jar or a pitcher. Add the spices and herbs. Sweeten to taste with sugar. Let stand for at least 12 hours. Strain before serving.

HOT SPICED WINE PUNCH

This hot spiced wine punch could well be a twentieth-century descendant of the punch that Gulielma Penn recorded.

1 cup sugar
4 cinnamon sticks
3 lemon slices
2 cups pineapple juice
2 cups orange juice
6 cups dry red wine
½ cup dry sherry
2 lemons, sliced

In a small saucepan, combine the sugar, cinnamon sticks, 3 lemon slices, and ½ cup water. Cook over low heat, stirring frequently, until the sugar dissolves. Boil for 5 minutes, then remove the pan from the heat and strain the syrup. Discard the cinnamon sticks and lemon slices.

In a large pot, combine the pineapple juice, orange juice, dry red wine, and sherry. Heat over low heat. Do not allow the mixture to boil. Stir in the syrup.

Serve hot, garnished with the lemon slices.

Gifts From Your Kitchen

*W*hether simple or elaborate, sweet or savory, gifts from a Christmas kitchen offer a special measure of caring. It is in the joyous spirit of the season to share good things with those you love—to prepare heirloom recipes from long-ago Christmases, indulge favorite tastes, please family and friends. Making and giving homemade cookies, breads, jellies, and other festive delights is a gift of yourself beyond price. A gift from your kitchen shows the extra thought and time you put into creating a special present. You need not be a gourmet cook to give homemade delicacies. Simple toasted, spiced nuts in a pretty tin will be appreciated as much as a loaf of fresh bread delivered still warm to a neighbor's door. It is an expression of the essential thoughtfulness of the holiday season that—beribboned and generous—conveys hearty best wishes now and in the days ahead.

Walnut Applesauce Loaf

This moist, not-too-sweet tea bread is so delicious you'll want to make extras to keep on hand for unexpected guests. It freezes well, so it can be made ahead of time.

½ cup butter, softened
1 cup sugar
2 eggs
2 ounces unsweetened chocolate
1 teaspoon vanilla extract
1¾ cups sifted cake flour
1½ teaspoons baking powder
½ teaspoon baking soda
½ teaspoon salt
½ teaspoon ground cinnamon
1 cup applesauce
½ cup broken walnuts

Makes 1 loaf

Preheat the oven to 325 degrees. Grease and flour a 9x5-inch loaf pan and set aside.

In a large bowl, cream the butter while gradually adding the sugar. Add the eggs, one at a time, beating well after each addition.

In the top of a double boiler, combine the chocolate and the vanilla extract. Cook over simmering water, stirring constantly, until the chocolate has melted and the mixture is smooth. Remove from the heat and set aside to cool.

Into a large bowl sift together the flour, baking powder, baking soda, salt, and cinnamon.

Blend the cooled chocolate into the batter. Then stir in large spoonfuls of the flour mixture alternating with the applesauce. Stir in the nuts.

Pour the batter into the prepared pan. Bake for 1 hour and 10 minutes, or until a cake tester comes out clean.

Cool the loaf in the pan on a wire rack for 15 minutes. Remove the loaf from the pan and return the loaf to the rack to cool completely.

Poppy Seed Tea Loaf

Moist and golden, this sweet bread can be made weeks ahead and frozen until gift-giving time.

3 cups all-purpose flour
1 teaspoon salt
1½ teaspoons baking powder
2¼ cups sugar
3 eggs, lightly beaten
1½ cups milk
1⅛ cups cooking oil
1½ tablespoons poppy seeds
1½ teaspoons vanilla extract
1½ teaspoons almond extract

Glaze (optional)
¼ cup orange juice
½ cup sugar
½ teaspoon vanilla extract
½ teaspoon almond extract
½ teaspoon butter flavoring

Makes 2 large or
3 small loaves

Preheat the oven to 350 degrees. Lightly grease and flour two large or three small loaf pans.

In a large bowl, combine the flour, salt, baking powder, and sugar. Mix well, then stir in the eggs, milk, and oil. Add the poppy seeds, vanilla extract, and almond extract. Beat with an electric mixer for 2 minutes. Do not overbeat.

Pour the batter into the prepared pans. Bake for 50 to 60 minutes, or until a cake tester comes out clean.

While the loaves are baking make the glaze, if desired. In a small bowl, combine all the ingredients for the glaze and mix well. Pour glaze over the loaves while they are still warm. Allow the loaves to cool in the pans.

Old-Fashioned Date-Nut Loaf

Date-Nut Loaf is a Christmas classic, but it tastes good any time of the year. It is particularly nice with Ginger Cream Cheese so you might want to give a Date-Nut Loaf and a jar of Ginger Cream Cheese in a small gift basket.

8 ounces pitted dates, coarsely chopped
4 tablespoons unsalted butter, softened
½ cup sugar
1 egg
1 teaspoon vanilla extract
1½ cups all-purpose flour
1 teaspoon baking soda
½ teaspoon ground mace
Pinch of salt
½ cup coarsely chopped walnuts
Walnut halves

Makes 1 loaf

Preheat the oven to 325 degrees. Grease an 8x4-inch loaf pan.

Put the dates in a bowl and add boiling water to cover. Set aside.

In a large mixing bowl, cream together the butter and the sugar. Beat in the egg and the vanilla extract. Combine 1 cup of flour with the baking soda, mace, and salt, and stir into the butter and sugar mixture. Stir in the dates and the water in which they soaked. In a small bowl, combine the walnuts and the remaining ½ cup of flour. Mix well to coat the walnuts with flour, then stir into the batter.

CHECKERBOARD SQUARES

5 ounces unsweetened chocolate
1 cup unsalted butter
2 cups sugar
4 eggs
1 cup flour, sifted
1 tablespoon vanilla extract
1 cup coarsely chopped pecans
1 cup raisins or dried currants

FROSTING

3 ounces semisweet chocolate
1 tablespoon unsalted butter,
    softened
3 ounces white chocolate
¼ cup heavy cream

Makes two
8-inch-square cakes

Preheat the oven to 350 degrees. Line two 8-inch-square baking pans with lightly buttered foil.

In a large, heavy saucepan, combine the unsweetened chocolate and the butter. Cook over very low heat, stirring frequently, until the chocolate and butter are melted. Add the sugar, stirring until the ingredients are well blended. Add the eggs, one at a time, beating after each addition. Stir in the flour. Remove the pan from the heat and beat in the vanilla extract. Pour half of the batter into a bowl. Mix the pecans into that batter, then spoon it into one of the pans. Mix the raisins, or dried currants, into the remaining batter and pour it into the other pan.

Bake for 25 minutes, or just until the center of each cake is firm to the touch. Do not overbake. Cool the cakes in the pans on wire racks.

When the cakes are quite cool, in a small saucepan, melt

Pour the batter into the prepared loaf pan. Decorate the top of the loaf with several walnut halves. Bake for 40 to 50 minutes, or until a cake tester comes out clean.

Let the loaf cool in the pan on a wire rack.

CRANBERRY NUT BREAD

2 cups flour, sifted
¾ cup sugar
3 teaspoons baking powder
¼ teaspoon salt
1 cup coarsely chopped cranberries
½ cup chopped walnuts
2 eggs
1 cup milk
¼ cup butter, melted
1 teaspoon vanilla extract

Makes 2 loaves

Preheat the oven to 350 degrees. With butter, grease 2 foil 7x4x3-inch loaf pans.

Into a large bowl, sift together the flour, sugar, baking powder, and salt. Stir in the cranberries and the walnuts. Make a well in the center.

In another large bowl combine the eggs, milk, melted butter, and vanilla extract. Using an electric mixer, beat until the ingredients are well blended. Pour into the well in the flour mixture. Stir just until the dry ingredients are moistened. Spoon the batter into the two prepared pans. Place the pans on a baking sheet. Bake for 40 to 45 minutes.

Cool the loaves in the pans for 10 minutes, then remove them from the pans and place on a wire rack to cool.

the semisweet chocolate over very low heat. Stir in the softened butter. Remove the pan from the heat and set aside. In another small saucepan, combine the white chocolate, broken into pieces, and the heavy cream. Cook over very low heat, stirring constantly until the chocolate has melted and the mixture is smooth. Set aside to cool slightly.

Carefully turn the cakes out of their pans and peel off the foil. Frost one cake with the dark chocolate, the other with the white chocolate. Let stand until the frosting is firm.

Cut each cake into sixteen even squares. Re-form the cakes, alternating dark and light squares. Cover and store in a cool place.

HARVEST TART

This wonderful pie is as decorative as it is delicious. And it is not difficult to make.

1 cup pitted prunes
1 cup dried apricots
2 cups peeled and chopped baking apples
½ cup golden raisins
⅓ cup granulated sugar
½ cup chopped walnuts
¼ cup butter, melted
⅔ cup Grand Marnier
Pastry for one 9-inch double crust
1 egg, beaten

Makes one 9-inch pie

Preheat the oven to 350 degrees. In a large saucepan, combine the prunes, apricots, apples, and raisins. Add water just to cover the fruit. Simmer over moderate heat, stirring occasionally, until the fruit is tender, about 20 minutes. Drain the fruit and then chop it coarsely.

In a saucepan, combine the fruit, sugar, walnuts, melted butter, and Grand Marnier. Bring to a simmer and cook for 5 minutes, stirring occasionally. Set aside to cool to room temperature.

Roll out half of the pastry dough and use it to line a 9-inch pie pan. Spoon in the filling, mounding it slightly. Roll out the remaining dough to a 10½-inch round and cut into ½-inch strips. Weave the strips lattice-fashion over the filling. Trim the ends and decoratively crimp the edges of the pie crust. Brush the lattice top with the beaten egg. Bake for 30 to 35 minutes, or until the top is golden and the filling is bubbling.

CRANBERRY TART

1 envelope gelatin
¼ cup cold water
¼ cup Frangelico
¾ cup sugar
½ cup seedless raspberry preserves
3 cups fresh cranberries
10-inch tart crust (recipe follows)

Makes one 10-inch tart

In a small saucepan combine the gelatin, water, and Frangelico. Cook over low heat, stirring constantly, until the gelatin dissolves. Combine the raspberry preserves and sugar in another saucepan and cook over low heat, stirring, until the sugar dissolves. Add the cranberries and cook for 10 minutes. Remove the pan from the heat, cool slightly, then stir in the gelatin mixture. Pour the cranberry mixture into the prepared crust. Chill until serving.

CRUST

⅔ cups unsalted butter
2 cups flour
1 teaspoon salt
⅓ cup ice water

In a food processor, combine the butter, flour, and salt. Process until the flour resembles coarse cornmeal. Add the ice water and process until the mixture forms a ball. Cover and chill for 1 hour.

Preheat the oven to 350 degrees. Roll the dough out on a floured board and fit into a 10-inch tart pan. Prick with a fork. Line with foil and place pie weights (or dried beans) on top. Bake for 15 to 20 minutes until lightly browned. Remove the pie weights and foil. Let the crust cool before adding the filling.

PAIN D'ÉPICE

The fine texture of this French spice bread depends on long and vigorous beating—in an electric mixer set at medium speed for 20 minutes, or with a wooden spoon for as long as your arm holds out. This tea bread is well worth the effort. It should be sliced thin and served with unsalted butter.

3 cups unbleached flour
1 cup rye flour
2 teaspoons salt
2 teaspoons baking powder
2 teaspoons baking soda
¼ teaspoon powdered anise
1 teaspoon ground cinnamon
2 teaspoons ground ginger
1 cup honey, strained
2 eggs, slightly beaten
2 cups milk

Makes 2 loaves

Preheat the oven to 350 degrees. Generously butter two 9x5-inch loaf pans.

Into a large mixing bowl sift together the flours, salt, baking powder, baking soda, powdered anise, cinnamon, and ginger. Stir in the honey, eggs, and milk. Beat until the mixture is very light and smooth.

Spoon the batter into the prepared loaf pans, and bake for about 50 minutes. Turn the loaves out on a wire rack. When they cool completely, wrap them tightly in foil and store them in the refrigerator. They may also be frozen.

PULL-APARTS

Arrange this coffee cake on an antique breadboard for an impressive gift for a busy household. It can be made several weeks ahead and frozen until gift-giving time.

2 packages active dry yeast
½ cup warm water
½ cup milk, scalded, then
    cooled to lukewarm
½ cup sugar
½ cup butter, softened
1 teaspoon salt
2 eggs
4½ to 5 cups all-purpose flour

CINNAMON GLAZE
1 cup sugar
1 tablespoon ground cinnamon
½ cup butter, melted

Makes 1 coffee cake

In a large bowl, dissolve the yeast in the warm water. Stir in the milk, sugar, salt, butter, and eggs. Mix well. Stir in 2½ cups of flour and beat until the dough is smooth. Mix in enough remaining flour to make the dough easy to handle. Turn the dough out onto a lightly floured board and knead it until it is smooth and elastic. If the dough becomes sticky while kneading, dust the board with additional flour.

Place the dough in a greased bowl, turning it to coat the entire surface. Cover the bowl, put it in a warm place, and let the dough rise until it is double in size—about 1½ hours.

Punch the dough down. Pull off pieces of the dough and form them into balls about 1½ inches in diameter.

With butter, generously grease a bundt pan or ring mold.

Make the cinnamon glaze: in a small bowl combine the sugar and the cinnamon. Pour the melted butter into another bowl. Dip each dough ball into the melted butter, turning to coat it, and then dip it into the cinnamon mixture. In the prepared pan, arrange the balls in a single layer so they just touch. Top with another layer. Continue until all the dough balls are used. Set aside in a warm place until the dough rises again to double its size.

Preheat the oven to 375 degrees.

Bake the coffee cake for 35 to 40 minutes. Remove the pan from the oven. Place a plate over the pan and invert it, allowing the cinnamon glaze to drizzle down over the coffee cake.

When serving, Pull-Aparts can be broken off with a fork or fingers. To freeze, allow cake to cool completely, then wrap it securely in 2 layers of aluminum foil.

CHRISTMAS BREAD

This delicious Christmas bread is a treat for Christmas morning, and it makes a gift that will truly be appreciated. It freezes well if it is well wrapped, so it can be made several weeks in advance.

1½ cups milk
½ cup unsalted butter
½ cup lukewarm water
1 tablespoon yeast
pinch of sugar
3 eggs
½ cup honey
5 to 7 cups unbleached white flour
1 teaspoon ground cinnamon
½ teaspoon ground nutmeg
½ teaspoon ground allspice
½ cup raisins
½ cup currants
1 teaspoon grated lemon peel
1 egg, beaten
Sliced almonds

Makes 3 loaves

In a small saucepan combine the milk and the butter. Cook over low heat, stirring frequently, until the butter melts and the milk is warm.

In a large mixing bowl, add the yeast and a pinch of sugar to the lukewarm water. Set aside until the yeast gets frothy, 5 to 10 minutes.

In another large bowl, beat the eggs. Pour in the warm milk and butter mixture. (If the milk is too hot, the eggs will curdle.) Stir in the honey, then 1 cup of flour. Using a large wooden spoon, beat 100 times. Add the cinnamon, nutmeg, allspice, raisins, currants, and the grated lemon peel. Beat another 25 times. Add the flour, one cup at a time, mixing well after each

addition, until the dough is a fairly solid mass. Turn the dough out on a large floured board and continue to add flour while kneading the dough until its texture is smooth and elastic.

Place the dough in a warm, buttered bowl. Cover the bowl, and put it in a warm place for 1 to 2 hours, or until the dough has doubled in bulk. Punch the dough down, return it to the bowl, cover, and set aside for another 1 to 2 hours, or until it has again doubled in bulk.

Turn the dough out onto a floured board and knead again. If the dough seems sticky add a little more flour. Divide the dough in thirds. Shape the dough into 3 round loaves or divide each portion into thirds and braid. After the loaves are shaped, brush them with the beaten egg and sprinkle the tops with the sliced almonds. Keep the loaves in a warm place for 30 minutes, or until they have almost doubled in bulk.

Preheat the oven to 350 degrees.

Bake 40 to 50 minutes for a braided loaf, 60 to 70 minutes for a round loaf.

BRIOCHE

4½ cups all-purpose flour, sifted
    before measuring
6 eggs at room temperature
1 teaspoon salt
1 cup unsalted butter, softened
½ cup warm water
1 package active dry yeast
2 tablespoons sugar
1 egg, well beaten

Makes 1 loaf

Place 3 cups of flour, the eggs, salt, and butter in the bowl of an electric mixer. Beat at medium speed for 2 minutes. In a separate small bowl dissolve the yeast in warm water (105 degrees) and add the sugar. When the yeast begins to bubble, pour it into the flour mixture and continue beating for 3 minutes.

Add the remaining flour and beat at low speed until the dough is smooth. Cover the bowl with plastic wrap and a damp towel. Let rise in a warm place until the dough has doubled in bulk. Punch down, then refrigerate the dough overnight, covered with plastic wrap and weighted down with a plate.

Unwrap the dough, knead it on a floured surface and fit it into a large brioche pan. Cover and let rise. Preheat the oven to 375 degrees.

Brush the brioche with the beaten egg. Bake for 1 hour, or until the brioche has a hollow sound when tapped.

BAKED CARAMEL CORN

A favorite of everyone's childhood, caramel corn is a special holiday sweet.

6 quarts popped corn
1 cup shelled pecans or peanuts
2/3 cup plus 1 tablespoon butter
2 cups brown sugar, firmly packed
½ cup light corn syrup
1 teaspoon salt
½ teaspoon baking soda
1 teaspoon vanilla extract

Makes 6 quarts

Preheat the oven to 225 degrees. In a large bowl, combine the popped corn and nuts. Grease a very large roasting pan with 1 tablespoon of butter.

In a 1½-quart saucepan, melt the remaining butter. Stir in the brown sugar, corn syrup, and salt. Bring the mixture to a boil, stirring constantly. Continue to boil over medium heat, without stirring, for 5 minutes. Remove the pan from the heat and stir in the baking soda and the vanilla extract.

Gradually pour the hot syrup over the popped corn and nut mixture. Mix well.

Turn the coated corn into the prepared pan. Bake uncovered for 30 minutes, stirring after 15 minutes. Remove the pan from the oven. When the caramel corn has cooled completely break it into pieces. Store in airtight containers.

CHOCOLATE BONBON BOX

Cut out and have ready a pattern cut from paper, using the following measurements:

Bottom and cover (2) 6 x 3½"
Bottom sides (2) 5½ x 1"
Box ends (2) 3 x 1"

Temper 2 pounds of dark chocolate (see page 142) and spread evenly ⅛ inch thick on baking paper. When the chocolate is "dry" but not completely set, use the pattern to cut out two of each of the box parts with a sharp knife. "Glue" the pieces together with melted chocolate. When set, brush the box with tempered chocolate. Fill the box with chocolates or other goodies.

CHRISTMAS TREES

If desired you can decorate these Christmas trees by drizzling "snow" made from tempered white chocolate over them in a lacy pattern and adding bits of colored fruit or candies.

1 cup powdered sugar
1 cup shortening
2 cups melted dark chocolate
½ cup kirsch
Makes 6

In a large bowl, whip the powdered sugar and shortening together. Add the melted dark chocolate and stir until blended. Add the kirsch. Using a pastry bag with a wide tip, pipe trees onto a lightly greased baking sheet: holding the bag upright with the tip almost touching the sheet, squeeze out a 1½-inch round of chocolate; lift the bag slightly and squeeze out a second, slightly smaller round of chocolate onto the first; repeat with a third, even smaller round, then lift the tip of the pastry bag straight up so the "tree" ends in a point.

NUTMEG TRUFFLES

These luscious nutmeg truffles should be stored in the refrigerator.

1 cup heavy cream
1 stick unsalted butter
2 pounds milk chocolate, grated
½ large nutmeg, grated
¾ pound dark chocolate, grated
  and tempered (see page 142)
Powdered sugar
Makes about 4 dozen

In a heavy saucepan, melt the butter in the cream. Stir in the grated milk chocolate and nut-

meg. When the chocolate has melted and the mixture is smooth, spread it to a ½-inch thickness on a cookie sheet. When it has cooled, cut it into ½-inch cubes. Roll the cubes into balls. Chill.

Dip the truffles once in the tempered chocolate. Then dip each one a second time, roll it immediately in powdered sugar, then score with the tines of a fork so the balls resemble nutmegs.

AMARETTO TRUFFLES

These truffles may be the quintessential candy. Very rich, they are an elegant gift.

12 ounces semisweet chocolate
½ cup butter
2 egg yolks
½ cup heavy cream
¼ cup amaretto
Finely chopped almonds
Cocoa
Makes about 4 dozen

In the top of a double boiler, over simmering water, melt the chocolate, stirring frequently. Remove the whole double boiler from the heat and add the butter, 1 tablespoon at a time, stirring until it has melted and the mixture is smooth.

In a small bowl, beat the egg yolks until they are thick and lemon colored. Gradually stir about ¼ of the hot chocolate mixture into the beaten yolks, then add the yolk mixture to the remaining hot chocolate mixture, stirring constantly. Stir in the heavy cream and the amaretto.

Return the double boiler to the heat. Cook, stirring con-

HOW TO TEMPER CHOCOLATE

Chocolate must be tempered so it will not separate when it is melted. It is not difficult to do, but to ensure success, use a candy thermometer.

Grate the amount of chocolate needed, and heat ⅔ of it in a double boiler (make sure the upper pan is over, not in, hot water) to 110 degrees on a candy thermometer. Do not overheat. Cool the chocolate to 75 degrees by adding the remaining ⅓ of grated chocolate, and stir thoroughly until the chocolate melts and is smooth. Carefully reheat the chocolate to 91 to 93 degrees, stirring constantly to avoid overheating.

TO TEMPER CHOCOLATE FOR COATING

Grate the chocolate and melt ⅔ of it in a double boiler, being careful that it does not get hotter than 110 degrees. Cool to 75 degrees by adding the remaining ⅓ grated chocolate. Carefully reheat over hot water to 98 degrees, stirring constantly to avoid overheating.

stantly, until the water comes to a simmer. Then cook, stirring, for 1 minute or until the mixture is smooth and thickened. Remove the top of the double boiler and set aside until the mixture has cooled, then cover it and refrigerate overnight, or until the mixture is firm enough to shape into 1-inch balls.

Roll the truffles in the finely chopped almonds or the cocoa. Or roll half in the almonds and the other half in the cocoa. Store the truffles in a covered container in the refrigerator. Serve chilled.

GIANDUJA BARS
1 pound hazelnuts, roasted and peeled
¾ pound sugar
4 tablespoons vegetable oil
1 pound dark chocolate, melted
2 cups hazelnuts, roasted, peeled, and coarsely chopped

Makes 36 bars

Place the 1 pound of roasted hazelnuts, the sugar, and the oil in the bowl of a food processor. Process to a smooth paste. Add the melted chocolate and chopped nuts and mix thoroughly. Spread the mixture evenly, about 1-inch thick, on a cookie sheet and allow to cool. While still soft, cut into bars. Store in the refrigerator.

CHOCOLATE BARK

Fill pretty holiday tins with this easy-to-prepare sweet. Store them in the refrigerator until you are ready to present them. White chocolate can be substituted for the semisweet chocolate if desired.

*1 pound good quality semisweet
    chocolate*
1 tablespoon margarine
1 cup pecans, coarsely chopped
1 cup raisins

Makes 1¼ pounds

Line a jelly-roll pan with buttered wax paper and set aside.

In the top of a double boiler over hot, not boiling water, melt the chocolate. Add the margarine and stir until the mixture is smooth and well blended. Spread half of the chocolate in a thin, even layer on the wax paper. Sprinkle the chocolate with the pecans and the raisins. Spoon the remaining chocolate evenly over the top. Chill the bark, covered, in the refrigerator for 3 to 4 hours, or until it is hard. Break into irregular pieces. Store in an airtight tin in the refrigerator.

CHOCOLATE LEAVES

These chocolates look wonderful and are surprisingly easy to make. Store them in the refrigerator in an airtight container, with pieces of wax paper between each layer.

30 holly leaves
6 ounces semisweet chocolate

Makes 30 leaves

Wash and dry the holly leaves. Line a baking sheet with wax paper.

In the top of a double boiler over hot, not boiling water, melt the chocolate. With a table knife, coat the back of each leaf with the melted chocolate, making sure to leave a thick spine and not to spread the chocolate onto the front of the leaf. Place the leaves chocolate-side up on the prepared baking sheet. Refrigerate until the chocolate is firm. To remove the leaf from the chocolate, pull gently on the leaf stem. The chocolate and the leaf will separate.

CHOCOLATE-DIPPED DRIED APRICOTS

Apricots have long been a traditional part of Christmas celebrations. A tin of these elegant sweetmeats will be appreciated by everyone—either for entertaining or sheer self-indulgence.

1 cup sugar
²/3 cup water
48 dried apricot halves
*6 ounces good quality semisweet
    chocolate*
2 tablespoons apricot brandy
1 tablespoon vegetable shortening
2 tablespoons water

Makes 4 dozen

Spread a large sheet of waxed paper on a flat surface. Line a baking sheet with another sheet of wax paper and put it into the refrigerator.

In a medium-size saucepan, combine the sugar and the ²/3 cup of water. Cook over moderate heat, stirring constantly, until the sugar dissolves. Bring the syrup to a boil and cook, stirring occasionally, for 5 minutes. Reduce the heat and add the apricot halves. Mix well so the apricots are coated with the syrup. Simmer gently over low heat for 2 minutes. Using a slotted spoon, transfer the apricots to the wax paper.

In the top of a double boiler set over simmering water, combine 2 ounces of the chocolate, the apricot brandy, shortening, and 2 tablespoons of water. Cook, stirring constantly, until the chocolate has melted and the mixture is smooth. Add the remaining 4 ounces of chocolate, and continue stirring until the mixture is again smooth. Use a candy thermometer to check that the chocolate does not heat over 96 degrees.

Dip each apricot halfway into the chocolate mixture, when all the apricots have been dipped, put the baking sheet into the refrigerator to harden them. Store the apricots in airtight containers in the refrigerator.

BOURBON BALLS

These delectable confections are surprisingly easy to make. They must be stored in a cool place or in the refrigerator. To the chocolate that may be left over after dipping the bourbon balls, stir in enough raisins or peanuts to just coat them. Drop from a teaspoon onto wax paper and chill.

1 cup chopped pecans
¼ cup bourbon
1 pound powdered sugar, sifted
½ cup butter, melted
8 ounces unsweetened chocolate
1 tablespoon unsalted butter

Makes about 100 balls

Put the pecans into a small bowl. Add the bourbon and mix well. Set aside for 3 hours.

Cover two baking sheets with wax paper. Set aside.

Drain the pecans and put them into a large bowl. Add the powdered sugar and the melted butter and mix well. Make ¾-inch balls, arrange them on the prepared baking sheets and chill for 30 minutes.

In the top of a double boiler over gently simmering water, combine the chocolate and the tablespoon of butter. Cook, stirring, until the chocolate has melted and the mixture is smooth. Using a wooden pick, dip each chilled bourbon ball into the chocolate. Return the balls to the baking sheets and chill until firm.

PEPPERMINT CREAMS

These creamy candies look pretty when red or green food coloring is added. They can also be decorated with tiny green leaves. Store them in an airtight container between layers of wax paper.

2 cups granulated sugar
¼ cup light corn syrup
¼ cup milk
¼ teaspoon cream of tartar
½ teaspoon peppermint flavoring
Red or green food coloring (optional)

Spread a large sheet of wax paper on a flat work surface.

In a heavy saucepan, combine the sugar, corn syrup, milk, and cream of tartar. Cook over low heat, stirring constantly, until the sugar is dissolved.

Increase the heat to moderate and continue cooking, stirring constantly, until the mixture reaches the soft-ball stage (238 degrees on a candy thermometer). Remove the pan from the heat and set aside for about 3 minutes to allow the mixture to cool slightly.

Beat in the peppermint flavoring and a few drops of food coloring, if desired. Continue beating until the mixture is creamy.

Drop the candy by teaspoonfuls onto the waxpaper. When the peppermint creams have cooled completely store them in an airtight container.

NOUGAT CANDY

2 cups sugar
¾ cup heavy cream
1 cup milk
2 tablespoons light corn syrup
⅛ teaspoon salt
1 teaspoon vanilla extract
1 cup very coarsely chopped nuts

Makes about 1½ pounds

Butter an 11x7-inch pan.

In a heavy saucepan, combine the sugar, cream, milk, corn syrup, and salt. Cook over moderate heat, stirring constantly, until the mixture reaches the soft-ball stage, 240 degrees on a candy thermometer. Remove the pan from the heat. Add the vanilla and beat until the mixture is creamy. Mix in the nuts. Pour the nougat into the prepared pan. Cut the nougat into squares.

PECAN PRALINES

Pralines studded with pecans are a perennial favorite. If you prefer large patties, drop the pralines from a tablespoon. If you prefer them smaller, use a teaspoon. When the pralines have cooled completely, they may be stored in an airtight container between layers of wax paper.

4 cups firmly packed light brown sugar
⅔ cup half-and-half
2 tablespoons unsalted butter
⅛ teaspoon salt
2 cups coarsely chopped pecans

Spread a large sheet of wax paper on a work surface.

In a large, heavy saucepan combine the sugar, half-and-half, butter, and salt. Cook over high heat, stirring constantly until the sugar is dissolved.

Reduce the heat to moderate and continue cooking, without stirring, until the mixture comes to a boil. In the meantime, fill a pan into which the saucepan will fit with water. Bring the water to a boil, then turn off the heat.

When the sugar mixture comes to a boil, begin stirring constantly. Boil for 4 minutes, then stir in the nuts.

Put the saucepan over the hot water while dropping the pralines from a spoon onto the wax paper.

CHOCOLATE BONBONS

Neither cakes nor candies, but something quite delicious in between, these bonbons will keep in the refrigerator for up to one week, or they can be frozen.

6 ounces good quality semisweet chocolate
5 tablespoons unsalted butter
½ cup sugar
2 eggs, lightly beaten
½ cup all-purpose flour
½ teaspoon baking powder
1 teaspoon vanilla extract
1 cup chopped almonds
Halved almonds

CREAMY FROSTING
1 egg yolk
½ cup whipping cream
¾ cup sugar
3 ounces unsweetened chocolate
2 tablespoons unsalted butter, softened
1 teaspoon vanilla extract

Makes 55 to 60
Preheat the oven to 375 degrees. Line 1½-inch miniature muffin cups with bonbon papers. Put the muffin cups on baking sheets.

In the top of a double boiler over hot water, combine the chocolate and the butter. Stir until the chocolate and butter have melted and the mixture is smooth. Remove the top of the double boiler and stir in the sugar. Add the eggs and mix well. Stir in the flour, baking powder, vanilla, and chopped almonds.

Spoon a small amount of the chocolate mixture into each prepared muffin cup, filling the cups ½ to ¾ full. Bake for 8

minutes. The bonbons will look soft and underbaked, but will become firm as they cool. Let them cool in the muffin cups.

Prepare the Creamy Frosting. Put the egg yolk into a small bowl and beat lightly. Set aside. In a small heavy saucepan, combine the cream and sugar. Bring to a boil over moderate heat, stirring constantly. Reduce the heat and simmer for 5 minutes, stirring frequently. Add the chocolate and stir until it melts. Stir a spoonful of the chocolate mixture into the egg yolk to warm it. Add the egg yolk mixture to the saucepan. Add the butter and stir until melted. Stir in the vanilla extract.

Spoon a little of the frosting over each bonbon. Decorate the tops of the bonbons with the almond halves.

STRAWBERRY HEARTS
¾ pound unsalted butter, softened
1¾ cups powdered sugar
1 egg
2 cups all-purpose flour, sifted
1 cup cornstarch
2 cups blanched almonds, finely chopped
½ cup strawberry jam

Makes about 4½ dozen
In a large bowl, cream together the butter and 1 cup of sugar until the mixture is light and fluffy. Add the egg and mix well. Combine the flour and the cornstarch and add to the creamed mixture. Mix in the almonds. Wrap the dough in plastic wrap and refrigerate overnight.

Roll the dough on lightly floured board to a ¼-inch thickness. Cut out an equal number of 1½- and 3-inch hearts. Place the cookies on an ungreased cookie sheet and chill for 45 minutes.

Preheat the oven to 325 degrees. Bake the cookies for 10 minutes, or until they are lightly browned. Cool on a wire rack.

While the cookies are still warm, place ¼ teaspoon of jam in the center of each 3-inch heart. Put the smaller heart on top, then sprinkle cookies with powdered sugar.

CANDY CANE COOKIES

¾ cup unsalted butter, softened
¾ cup sugar
1 egg
½ teaspoon vanilla extract
½ teaspoon peppermint extract
2 cups all-purpose flour
½ teaspoon salt
¼ teaspoon baking powder
⅓ cup flaked coconut
1 teaspoon red food coloring

Makes 16 large cookies

In a large bowl, cream together the butter and sugar. Beat in the egg and the vanilla and peppermint extracts.

Combine the flour, salt, and baking powder and stir into the creamed mixture. Divide the dough in half. Stir the coconut into one portion; blend the red food coloring into the other portion. Wrap each one in plastic wrap and chill for 1 hour.

Preheat the oven to 375 degrees. Divide each portion of dough into 16 balls. Keep half of the dough chilled until ready to use. Roll each ball into a 6-inch rope. For each cookie, pinch together one end of a red rope and one end of a white rope; twist ropes together and pinch the ends. Place on an ungreased cookie sheet. Bend one end around into a cane shape. Repeat with the remaining balls. Bake for 10 minutes. Transfer the cookies to wire racks to cool.

ALL-PURPOSE GINGERBREAD

This is the gingerbread to make for cookies, ornaments, and even for gingerbread houses. The dough may be made in advance and refrigerated in a plastic bag, but it should be removed in time to be brought to room temperature before shaping.

1 cup sugar
1 cup unsulfured molasses
1 cup butter, melted
5 cups all-purpose flour
1 teaspoon baking soda
1 teaspoon salt
1 teaspoon grated nutmeg
1 tablespoon ground ginger

In a large bowl, combine the sugar and molasses. Stir in the melted butter. Sift together the flour, baking soda, salt, nutmeg, and ginger. Gradually add the flour mixture to the sugar mixture. A mixer may be used, but the last cup of flour should be added by hand because the dough will be too heavy for a standard mixer's motor. Knead the dough until well blended. Place the dough in a plastic bag and allow it to remain at room temperature. Do not refrigerate the dough while using or it will become too stiff.

GINGERBREAD HOUSES

Roll the dough to ¾-inch thickness and transfer to a lightly greased baking sheet. Place the pattern on the dough and cut around the pieces. Carefully remove excess dough, which can be reused. Bake in a preheated 350-degree oven for 13 to 15 minutes. Remove from the oven and cool on the sheet for 5 min-

utes before transferring pieces to a rack to finish cooling.

GINGERBREAD COOKIES AND ORNAMENTS

Roll the dough to ¼- or ½-inch thickness, directly on a lightly greased cookie sheet. Cut out desired shapes, carefully removing excess dough, which can be rolled out and used again. For ornaments, make a small hole at the top center of each cookie. Bake in a preheated 350-degree oven for 8 to 10 minutes. Remove from the oven and cool on the cookie sheet for 5 minutes before removing cookies to a wire rack to cool completely.

SUGAR COOKIES

This recipe makes delicious cookies that can be cut into shapes for the holidays. They can be decorated with Royal Icing, or sprinkled with red and green sugar. And the dough can be made in advance and chilled in the refrigerator.

¾ cup unsalted butter
1 cup sugar
1 egg
1 teaspoon vanilla extract
2 cups all-purpose flour
½ teaspoon baking powder
½ teaspoon salt

Makes 3 dozen cookies

In a large mixing bowl, cream together the butter and sugar until the mixture is light and fluffy. Beat in the egg and the vanilla. Combine the flour, baking powder, and salt and add to the creamed mixture. Form the dough into two balls and cover with plastic wrap. Chill the dough for at least 2 hours.

Preheat the oven to 375 degrees. Lightly grease cookie sheets with butter. Roll the dough on a floured board and cut to desired shapes with cookie cutters. Bake the cookies for 10 minutes. Decorate with Royal Icing.

ROYAL ICING

4 egg whites
1 pound powdered sugar
½ teaspoon cream of tartar

Combine the egg whites, sugar, and cream of tartar in the bowl of an electric mixer. Beat on low speed until the mixture forms a paste. Beat the icing on medium speed for 5 to 10 minutes until stiff peaks form. Cover the icing with a damp cloth to keep it from hardening. Remove small amounts to use as needed, adding drops of food coloring if desired.

LIZZIES

Easier to make and to serve than fruitcake, Lizzies are a favorite Christmas tradition in many families. Moist and rich, these cookies keep well in an airtight tin or they can be frozen.

½ cup bourbon whiskey
3 cups seedless golden raisins
¼ pound butter, softened
½ cup light brown sugar, firmly packed
2 eggs
1½ cups sifted flour
1½ teaspoons baking soda
1½ teaspoons ground cinnamon
½ teaspoon ground cloves
½ teaspoon ground nutmeg
4 cups chopped pecans
½ pound citron, chopped
1 pound candied cherries

Makes 7 to 8 dozen

Combine the bourbon and the raisins in a bowl. Mix well, then set aside for at least 1 hour.

Preheat the oven to 325 degrees. Grease 2 baking sheets.

In a large bowl, cream together the butter and the sugar. Using a mixer to beat in the eggs, continue beating until the mixture is light and fluffy.

Into another large bowl, sift together the flour, baking soda, cinnamon, cloves, and nutmeg. Add the flour mixture to the butter mixture and beat until smooth and well blended. Stir in the pecans, citron, cherries, and soaked raisins. Mix well.

Drop teaspoons of the batter onto the prepared baking sheets. Bake for 15 minutes or until the cookies are firm to the touch. Cool the cookies on wire racks, then store them in airtight containers.

DATE-NUT BARS

8 ounces pitted dates, chopped
1 cup chopped raisins
1 cup finely chopped walnuts
1 teaspoon grated lemon peel
1½ teaspoons ground cinnamon
1 cup sugar
½ cup unsalted butter, softened
1 teaspoon vanilla extract
2 eggs
2 cups all-purpose flour
2 teaspoons baking powder
½ teaspoon salt
2 tablespoons orange juice
Powdered sugar

Makes 64 bars

Preheat the oven to 375 degrees. Grease 2 baking sheets.

In a large bowl, combine the dates, raisins, walnuts, lemon peel, and cinnamon. Add ¼ cup of the sugar and mix gently until the fruit is coated with sugar.

In another large bowl, combine the butter, the remaining ¾ cup of sugar, and the vanilla extract. Cream until light and fluffy. Beat in the eggs one at a time, mixing well after each addition. Stir in the flour, baking powder, salt, and orange juice. Add the date mixture. Stir until blended, but do not over mix. The dough will be very stiff.

Divide the dough into four portions. Shape two logs on each prepared baking sheet. Make logs about 12x2x½-inches. Bake for 15 minutes. Although they will be slightly brown, the logs will feel very soft and underdone. They will become firm as they cool.

Cool for 15 minutes. Cut diagonally into ¾-inch bars. Dust with powdered sugar.

MINCEMEAT CRESCENTS

Mincemeat has been enjoyed for centuries and was a pie staple during the harsh winters of colonial America. The rich mincemeat flavor of these cookies is a traditional taste of the holiday season.

½ cup butter, softened
1 3-ounce package cream cheese, softened
1 cup unsifted all-purpose flour
¾ cup mincemeat
¼ cup sugar
1 teaspoon ground cinnamon
        Makes about 3 dozen

In a large bowl, cream together the butter and cream cheese. When the mixture is well blended, add the flour and mix thoroughly. Gather the dough into a ball, wrap it in wax paper and chill for 1 to 2 hours.

Preheat the oven to 375 degrees.

On a lightly floured board, roll the dough to ⅛-inch thickness. Cut out rounds using a 2½- or 3-inch round cookie cutter. Put 1 teaspoon of mincemeat in the center of each round, fold it over, and press edges together. Place the crescents on an ungreased baking sheet. Bake for 12 to 15 minutes, or until the crescents are lightly browned.

In a shallow bowl, combine the sugar and cinnamon. Mix well. As soon as the cookies are cool enough to handle roll them in the sugar mixture. Then put them on wire racks to cool. Store in the refrigerator.

CRANBERRY CONSERVE

This cranberry conserve makes a nice change from cranberry sauce or jelly. It is also a tasty addition to a turkey sandwich. Stored in sealed, sterile jars, it will keep in the refrigerator for up to six months.

4 cups fresh cranberries
1 cup raisins
1 orange, seeded and cut into small pieces
3 cups sugar
1½ cups chopped walnuts
        Makes 4 half-pints

Pick over and wash the cranberries. In a large saucepan, combine the cranberries with ⅔ cup cold water. Cook over moderate heat, stirring frequently, until the skins of the cranberries burst, about 10 minutes.

Push the cranberries through a strainer or food mill. Return the pureed cranberries to the saucepan with ⅔ cup boiling water, the raisins, orange, and sugar. Stirring frequently, bring the mixture to the boiling point, then reduce the heat and simmer for 20 minutes.

Remove the pan from the heat, stir in the walnuts, then set aside until the conserve is cool.

Spoon the conserve into sterile jars, seal, and store in the refrigerator.

GINGER WINTER RELISH

Sweet and tangy, this easy-to-make relish is a delightful addition to any dinner and perfect for a holiday ham or roast. It makes a fine addition to a gift basket.

2½ cups distilled white vinegar
2 cups sugar
2 cups golden raisins
2 cups dark raisins
⅓ cup coarsely chopped crystallized ginger
1 teaspoon red pepper flakes
2½ cups peeled, cored, and diced pears
2½ cups peeled, cored, and diced tart apples
1 large red bell pepper, seeded and diced

Makes 4 pints

In a large saucepan, combine the vinegar and sugar. Cook over moderate heat, stirring constantly until the sugar has dissolved. Stir in the raisins, ginger, and pepper flakes. Bring to a boil, then reduce the heat and simmer the mixture, stirring occasionally, for 5 minutes. Stir in the pears, apples, and bell pepper. Bring the mixture to a boil, then reduce the heat and simmer for 6 minutes, or until the fruit is only slightly soft.

This relish can be stored, covered, in the refrigerator for one month. To store it for a longer period of time it should be canned. To do this, pour the relish into canning jars, leaving ½-inch space at the top, and seal the lids according to the manufacturer's directions. Process in a hot water bath for 15 minutes.

HONEYED PEAR BUTTER

Fruit butters have been popular since colonial days. This pear butter can be made quickly, it can be stored in the refrigerator for up to 2 weeks, and it is a delicious spread for warm scones or slices of tea bread.

3 ripe but firm pears, peeled, cored, and chopped
½ cup water
1 tablespoon honey
1 teaspoon unsalted butter
½ teaspoon ground cinnamon

Makes 1 pint

In a saucepan, combine the pears, water, honey, butter, and cinnamon. Cook over medium heat, stirring frequently, for 15 to 20 minutes, or until the pears are tender. Remove the pan from the heat and set aside until the mixture has cooled to room temperature.

Drain the pears, discarding the liquid. Purée the pears, then transfer the purée to small containers. Store, covered, in the refrigerator.

APRICOT CREAM CHEESE

This spread is as flavorful as it is attractive. For giving, put it in a pretty jam pot.

3 ounces cream cheese, softened
1 tablespoon honey
1 cup drained and finely chopped canned apricots,
¼ cup finely chopped pecans or walnuts (optional)

Makes 1 cup

In a large bowl, using an electric mixer, blend the cream cheese and the honey until the mixture is smooth and fluffy. Stir in the chopped apricots and mix well. Stir in the nuts, if desired. Store, covered, in the refrigerator. Allow the cheese to soften for 30 minutes before serving.

GINGER CREAM CHEESE

For a thoughtful gift include a jar of this spread in a basket of quick breads. The cheese is equally delicious served with crisp apple and pear slices as an appetizer or a dessert.

8 ounces cream cheese, softened
2 tablespoons heavy cream
3 tablespoons (or to taste) finely chopped crystallized ginger
Toasted almond slivers

Makes 1 cup

In a large bowl, using an electric mixer, thoroughly blend the cream cheese and heavy cream. Stir in the crystallized ginger. Spoon the mixture into a jar or a small crock. Sprinkle with almond slivers. Cover and refrigerate. Before serving, allow the cheese to soften for 30 minutes.

MUSTARD FRUITS

When making this condiment for gift giving also make some for yourself to serve with the holiday turkey. It can be prepared days ahead and stored in the refrigerator.

2 cups ½-inch pieces cored and
    peeled pears
1 cup ½-inch pieces cored and
    peeled apple
1 cup ½-inch pieces cored and
    peeled pineapple
2 cups orange segments, pith
    removed
1 cup seedless grapes
½ cup sugar
1 teaspoon lemon extract
½ teaspoon vanilla extract
1 teaspoon turmeric
½ teaspoon ground allspice
3 teaspoons ground mustard powder
1 teaspoon vinegar
3 to 4 teaspoons all-purpose flour
Makes 2 pints

In a large saucepan combine the prepared pear, apple, and pineapple, the orange segments, and the grapes. Add enough water to cover the fruit half way, about 2 cups. Stir in the sugar, lemon extract, and vanilla extract. Bring to a boil over moderate heat, stirring frequently.

Meanwhile, in a small bowl, combine the turmeric, allspice, mustard, vinegar, and 3 teaspoons of flour. Stir until the mixture is a stiff paste. If necessary, add 1 more teaspoon of flour.

When the fruit mixture has come to a full boil, remove the pan from the heat. Strain the fruit and reserve the liquid. Set the fruit aside. Stir the liquid into the mustard paste.

Pour the mustard mixture into a large saucepan. Bring to a boil over moderate heat. Boil gently, stirring constantly, until the sauce thickens. Remove the pan from the heat. Fold the fruit into the sauce. Store, covered, in the refrigerator.

HORSERADISH JELLY

Valued since the days of ancient Greece and Rome for its medicinal properties and pungent flavor, horseradish enlivens many sauces and meat dishes. This honey-colored condiment is delicious with roast beef and chicken or served with cream cheese and crackers.

3¼ cups sugar
½ cup cider vinegar
½ cup prepared white horseradish
½ cup (1 pouch) liquid pectin
Makes 3 half-pints

In a large saucepan, combine the sugar, vinegar, and horseradish. Cook over moderate heat stirring constantly until the sugar dissolves. When the mixture reaches a boil, stir in all the pectin at once. Increase the heat, continue to stir and bring the mixture to a full rolling boil. Remove the pan from the heat and skim the foam off the top.

Pour immediately into hot, sterilized jelly jars. Adjust the lids to seal, according to the manufacturer's instructions.

LEMON CHUTNEY

The orange and yellow spicy chutney complements any kind of meat.

2 cups thinly sliced lemon
1 cup coarsely chopped dried
    apricots
1 cup golden raisins
1 cup finely chopped onions
1 cup sugar
1½ cups cider vinegar
3 tablespoons minced crystallized
    ginger
½ teaspoon crushed whole allspice
1 teaspoon salt
4 half-pints

In a heavy saucepan, combine all the ingredients. Bring to a boil over moderate heat, stirring frequently. Cover the pan, reduce the heat, and simmer the mixture for 1 hour, stirring occasionally. Remove the cover and simmer, stirring occasionally, for 30 minutes more, or until the mixture has thickened but is not dry.

Pour the chutney into hot sterilized jars leaving ½-inch space on top. Adjust the lids to seal according to the manufacturer's directions.

Index

Acknowledgments

Thanks to Leah Stamos for picture research, Jeanmarie Andrews for copyediting, and to those generous private homeowners, house museums, and historic restorations who allowed us to photograph, as well as to the collectors of Christmas past whose accumulations of treasure are shown on these pages. Most of all, thanks to Glorya Hale, who understands the pleasures of books.

Photography: David Bohl; John Corcoran; Brian Hunt; Bob Skalkowski; and Carl Socolow.
Heirlooms to Make: Adele Bishop (Stenciled Table Runner); Pat Broyles (Cornhusk Angel); Roberta Edrington (An Heirloom Santa); Dorothy Fillmore (Belsnickel Dummy Board).